# THE COLLECTED POEMS OF
# E. ETHELBERT MILLER

**Kirsten Porter, Ed.**

Willow Books, a division of AQUARIUS PRESS

*Detroit, Michigan*

The Collected Poems of E. Ethelbert Miller

Editor: Kirsten Porter

Cover design: "Recuento" by Felix Alberto Angel

ISBN 978-0-9961390-2-1

LCCN 2016935662

ESTABLISHED AUTHOR SERIES

WILLOW BOOKS, a division of AQUARIUS PRESS

www.WillowLit.net

Printed in the United States of America

For my children,

Jasmine-Simone Morgan and Nyere-Gibran Miller.

"The idea is not to live forever, it is to create something that will."

—*Andy Warhol*

# Table of Contents

VIII. <u>Whispers, Secrets and Promises</u> (Black Classic Press, 1998)

## Acknowledgments

We would like to thank Randall Horton and Aquarius Press for believing in the importance of this book. Our gratitude is extended to Paul Coates at Black Classic Press for giving some of the poems within this collection their first breath. We also owe thanks to the *Live to Give Charitable Trust* for providing Ethelbert the opportunity to work on this book.

Special thanks to Elisabeth Kaplan, Jennifer King, Christopher Walker in Special Collections Research at the Gelman Library for the time and care they put into archiving all of Ethelbert's papers.

Warm acknowledgments to those who gave their support to this project, especially: Michelle Blandburg, Heather Buchanan, John Cavanagh, Beverly Hunt, Charles Johnson, Holly Karapetkova, Denise King-Miller, Marguerite Rippy, and Myra Sklarew.

— *Ethelbert & Kirsten*

I wish to thank my teachers who encouraged my love of words: Gerri Hill, Gretchen Harris, Terri Matus, Lynn Siemon, Skip Bromley, Ron Shapiro, Jan Edmondson, Lisa Russ Sparr, Neva Herrington, Ellen Herbert, Sean Hoare, Jennifer Atkinson, and Eric Pankey. I am indebted to Lana Austin and Rebecca Cardon, dear friends who speak my language.

And most importantly, I thank my first teachers and biggest fans, my parents John and Donna Porter.

— *Kirsten*

# INTRODUCTION

*The Poetry of E. Ethelbert Miller:*
*Words to Grace a New Day*

I t is Friday, June 26, 2015, the day thousands of mourners gather to lay to rest Reverend Clementa Pinckney after he and eight of his parishioners were gunned down by a shooter during a bible study meeting. President Obama travels to Charleston to deliver the eulogy. Those who could not attend the funeral watch the service on their television and computer screens. It is another horrific and senseless loss, added to our country's swirling waters of hate crimes and violence. But on this day our President offers words of hope, "As a nation, out of this terrible tragedy, God has visited grace upon us for he has allowed us to see where we've been blind…He's given us the chance, where we've been lost, to find our best selves." And then in a move that would surprise those listening, Obama ends his eulogy with a rendition of "Amazing Grace" that brings the gathered crowd to its feet. The President's notes are not perfect, but the words he sings of grace and transformation are words we need to hear. It is a song our nation—and the world—needs to hear, now more than ever.

America needs a new song, new words that speak the language of our hearts. We need writers. We need poets. In an essay called "The Poet," published in the 1840s, Ralph Waldo Emerson extolled the poet's ability to articulate what is in the hearts of his people. The poet may produce poems about his own experience, but he is also charged with the duty to write poems that are representative of his community's experience. Emerson lamented that at the time he wrote his essay, there was no poet for America, no one to write the words on the hearts of a nation. And just as our country needed to hear the brave notes from President Obama's eulogy in the wake of tragedy, Emerson claimed America desperately needed poets to write new poems—"The men of more delicate ear write down these cadences more faithfully, and these transcripts, though imperfect, become the songs of the nations."

A poet is given the unique responsibility of composing the poems that become the songs of a nation, and I can think of no current poet better than E. Ethelbert Miller whose poems sing America's heart-song. Miller's poetry sings of the sadness, loneliness, and longing for spiritual and human connection found in an imperfect world. His words are a call for love and equality, a protest against oppression, a prayer for change. His language promotes compassion, healing, and amazing grace.

When Emerson made his plea for a poet to emerge who could sing for America, it was Walt Whitman who answered. Whitman had known he was destined to be a poet; he had received that "out of the cradle endlessly rocking" calling, no different than when a nun receives her divine calling from God. Miller, too, was struck with the realization that he was born to be a poet. He writes in his memoir *Fathering Words*:

> One night a poem comes to me. Words. Revelations...I start praying. Suddenly words are escorting me across the street. I reach the other side, proud of what I've done. I can write. My prayers are songs. I can make music. I can give color to the world. This is my life. This is my gift.

And Miller has already shared his gift. With a literary career that began in 1969, Miller has spent over forty years blessing us with his writings. The author of two memoirs and eleven books of poetry, Miller adds an important voice to the collective American experience. His poetry anthology *In Search of Color Everywhere* was awarded the 1994 PEN Oakland Josephine Miles Award. In 2003, his first memoir, *Fathering Words,* was selected by the D.C. Public Library for its DC WE READ, one book, one city program. Miller's words have extended beyond our borders to touch countless readers with translations of his poems appearing in Spanish, Portuguese, German, Hungarian, Chinese, Farsi, Norwegian, Tamil, and Arabic.

As a writer and literary activist, a large part of Miller's mission is to advocate for the arts and art education. From 1974-2015, Miller served as the director of the African American Resource Center at Howard University. He is a proactive member of organizations that promote collaboration between thinkers and visionaries and work for positive change in our nation and world. Miller is the founder and former chair of the Humanities Council of Washington, D.C. and served as a Commissioner for the D.C. Commission on the Arts and Humanities from 1997-2008. He is board emeritus for the PEN/ Faulkner Foundation and current board chair of the Institute for Policy Studies, a progressive think tank located in Washington, D.C.

An overwhelming number of writers and artists credit Miller for his selfless commitment to promote their careers. In 1974, Miller launched the *Ascension* Poetry Reading Series which he ran for over twenty-five years, providing a forum for hundreds of African American poets and poets of color to present their work to the general public. In 1997, Miller worked with the Inter-Governmental Philatelic Corporation and successfully lobbied for postage stamps issued by Ghana and Uganda to feature twelve prominent African American writers including Alex Haley, Zora Neale Hurston, and Richard Wright.

In recognition of his gifts as a writer and his efforts to advance the arts, Miller has received numerous accolades. City mayors proclaimed "E. Ethelbert Miller Day" in D.C. on September 28, 1978, and in Jackson, Tennessee on May 21, 2001. He received the Mayor's Arts Award in 1982 for Literature, the Public Humanities Award in 1988, and the Columbia Merit Award in 1994. Miller was made an honorary citizen of Baltimore on July 17, 1994. In 1996, the beloved poet was asked to give the commencement address at Emory and Henry College and was awarded an honorary degree of Doctor of Literature. In 2001 and 2003, Miller was honored at the National Book Festival hosted by Laura Bush. He has been a Fulbright Senior Specialist Program Fellow to Israel in 2004 and 2012. In February 2006, Miller was the keynote speaker at the 50th Anniversary of the Fulbright Program in Israel, at the Embassy of Israel in Washington, D.C. In February 2007, the poet was awarded the Barnes & Noble Writers for Writers Award by Poets and Writers. He has been awarded fellowships by the Virginia Center for Creative Arts and the Gaea Foundation. In 2015, Miller was inducted into the Washington, D.C. Hall of Fame.

Miller continues to work tirelessly as the editor of *Poet Lore*, the oldest poetry magazine published in the United States. He often appears on National Public Radio, and he hosts and produces *The Scholars*, a UDC-TV show that features interviews with emerging community talents. Miller writes his monthly column *E on DC* for Capital Community News, and he has been writing *E-Notes*, his widely-read blog, since 2004.

Miller is a treasure among the artistic community for his service and advocacy, but it is his poetic gifts that make him most qualified to sing America's song. His poems encompass despair, the helplessness we feel when Achebe's words "all things fall apart" prove to be all too devastatingly true:

> the sadness tonight is too heavy for eyes
> i cannot sleep
> stars fall and i witness the crumbling of heavens
> all things holy have been destroyed

> *—from "Samson," by E. Ethelbert Miller*

Miller writes of the daily injustices that occur in America. His poems ask us to heed Obama's words so that we may "see where we've been blind":

> ...no one told you about the black laws
> of cause and effect. Your science teacher
> failed to teach you about why a police
> club struck against a black man's head
> in the south resulted in a house burning
> down in the north or how prejudice could
> make a store clerk's smile turn into a
> coldness below freezing. You often
> wondered while waiting in line how you
> could become invisible to every atom in
> the world...

> *—from "Science," by E. Ethelbert Miller*

But Miller also embraces the celebratory in his poetry. He records those moments in our daily life that leave us in wonder:

> on my desk is a small bottle
> which once held perfume
> inside is the cord that joined
> my wife and daughter

> ...

> tomorrow when my daughter becomes a woman

i will give her this small bottle
filled with the beginnings of herself

on that day she will hold love
in her hands

*—from "Jasmine," by E. Ethelbert Miller*

Miller's poetry sings of a world where pain and joy coexist. He turns our tears over in his hands, he examines the small intimacies found in a touch between friends, an embrace between lovers. And in a world where senseless acts of violence occur, where the beautiful lives of nine people can be ended by the cruelty of one, Miller offers up a poem to help us move towards healing:

only language
can hold us together

i watch the women
bead their hair
each bead a word

braids becoming
sentences

…

i need to do something
about my hair

if only i could
remember

the words
to the language
that keeps
breaking in my
hands

*—from "Only Language Can Hold Us Together," by E. Ethelbert Miller*

Is our nation breaking? Or have we already been broken? Whichever the case, our poets of today have a daunting task; they must sing the stories of our truths, inspiring us to become our "best selves" and begin to heal our brokenness. They must write the poems that will "hold us together." And they must look inward and outward, choosing the words that are the chords of their experience that can also represent our nation.

> poetry is prayer
> light dancing inside words
>
> …
>
> I prepare to recite
> what is in my heart

*—from "Salat," by E. Ethelbert Miller*

Emerson once asked for a poet to take up the pen and proclaim, "It is in me," and then write poems to a country without a song. Do you hear America singing Whitman? We are waiting for a poet to answer the call once again. We are waiting for a new song.

E. Ethelbert Miller is that poet we have been waiting for. If you hold his words close to your ear, you will hear his poems sing the grace notes of a new day.

### Section Discussions

I. **Early Poems** (archives, personal collections, magazine publications, circa 1970s)

In the *Early Poems* section, readers are invited to walk along with Miller as he begins his journey as a writer. Born in 1950, Miller grew up in a Caribbean-American family in South Bronx, New York. His father, Egberto Miller, worked in the post office, and his mother, Enid Miller, worked in the garment industry. Miller is the youngest of three siblings; he idolized his older brother Richard and was close with his sister Marie. It was not until Miller moved away from home to attend Howard University, a historically black college in Washington, D.C., that he began to write in a more serious manner.

When Miller arrived at Howard in 1968, the United States was experiencing great turmoil and social upheaval. John Kennedy and Martin Luther King, Jr. had been assassinated. Riots spread throughout the country, while we were entrenched overseas in the Vietnam War. Many of these internal and outside conflicts were reflected on the Howard campus. Miller began college in the aftermath of a national student protest. Influenced by the Black Arts movement, Howard students had shut down the school the semester before Miller arrived on campus. One of the demands made by the students was for the university to offer an Afro American studies program. Miller would be one of the first students to major in Afro American studies at Howard.

Writing his first poems on the backs of envelopes for friends, Miller began sharing his poems more publicly at poetry readings in 1969. At this time, his first published poems were featured in *The Hilltop*, the school's newspaper founded by Zora Neale Hurston. Miller graduated from Howard in 1972. Most of the poems found in the *Early Poems* section were written when Miller was still a student at Howard University. While some of these poems were later published in magazines, they were not included in his eleven print or online poetry collection publications.

As the editor of this collection, I have a particular fondness for the pieces included in the *Early Poems*. The process of gathering these poems was a bit like embarking on a treasure hunt. Miller sent me many of these forgotten poems that he had found in his personal library. However, we discovered most of the early poems in the cold months of winter at the Gelman Library in Washington, D.C. Collected and archived under the name "The Papers of E. Ethelbert Miller," these early documents were meticulously organized by the Special Collections Research division at The George Washington University Library. While the snow fell outside, Miller and I sat inside poring over the treasures collected in boxes — his earliest letters, essays, and poems. Miller had composed many of these pieces on an old typewriter, so I took pictures of the poems we selected for inclusion and later inputted them on my computer. Readers who are already familiar with Miller's work will delight in this section that includes many poems never seen before.

In these early poems, we see a writer drinking in the cultural, religious, musical, and poetic offerings that he found available to him as a young college student living in the Cook Hall dorm at Howard. In 1974, Miller was named director of Howard's African-American Resource Center. This position put the young poet at the center of the university's initiative to create a space for research involving American Black history and literature, as well as history from the African Diaspora.

Miller's early poems are shaped by cultural influences from the Black Arts Movement and writers like Amiri Baraka and Askia M. Touré. He was greatly inspired by his poetry mentors at Howard: Haki Madhubuti (then Don L. Lee), Stephen Henderson, and Sterling Brown. The young writer absorbed religious teachings found in Sufi writings, the Quran, and works by Thomas Merton. The music created by musicians who Miller grew up with—Paul Simon, Phil Ochs, Joan Baez, and Bob Dylan— became the background chords in his poetry. Even the signature short poem aesthetic of Miller's early work can be traced back to the kinds of poems he read at Howard in one of his favorite books, "Destination Ashes" by Norman Jordan.

You will notice in these early poems that Miller is experimenting with form and style. Like a child trying on different clothes in a dress-up box, the young writer plays with poem length, capitalization, and language. Many of these early poems are short, sometimes written in just a few lines, or in the case of "Indian Summer," one word stands alone for each of its twelve lines. With a few rare exceptions, each poem uses lowercase letters and virtually no punctuation. In a poem like "Candy" even the pronoun "you" is playfully truncated to "u." While he abandons shortening words in later sections, he holds onto the style of utilizing the lowercase and minimal punctuation. It is not until almost twenty-five years into Miller's writing career that we start to see more consistent forms of punctuation creep into his poems with the 1994 publication of Miller's sixth book "First Light." It would take another ten years with the 2004 publication of "How We Sleep on the Nights We Don't Make Love" before Miller would begin to drop the lowercase style. He explains his adoption of a more conservative approach in style as his attempt to preserve language in spite of its current decay. With today's overuse of slang and text-speak, Miller emphasizes even the poet's choice of including a comma or capitalizing a letter becomes important in the preservation of language.

The early poems selected for this book help to articulate Miller's principle thematic concerns, including love, isolation, depression, hunger for intimacy, spiritual longing, and human rights. These themes serve as a foundation for Miller's early work and evolve over the span of his career to inform much of his later poetry.

The *Early Poems* section includes several short poems that read like a whisper in a lover's ear:

Shirley

your hair alabama red
i leave tuskegee
with sunset eyes

This love is often fleeting, and when it falls away we are offered poems that ring with loneliness. Consider the quiet solitude of "Lone Journey into Midnight" as the speaker laments:

hands no longer
compose music
on my flesh at night
my bed is a coffin
making a midnight
journey to a final
resting place

Many of these early poems capture the difficulty of transition. We hear the melancholy in aging, the heartbreak in realizing the body is breaking down. But while the world is quick to overlook these "Old Men," Miller insists on seeing their faces and writing their truths:

their bodies still sweat
water
ripples
through
the wrinkles
in their
foreheads
sometimes
they will say a few
words when you pass
many times
they just bow their
heads
and stare quietly at
the ground

Such moments of despair and isolation fuel the poet's desire to find intimacy. We feel the painful ache for physical connection in the poem "Thirst":

> the dry ground cracking outside
> I hear it crying
>
> there are nights when the air cools
> and I think of you
>
> thirst holding me back

We also see an intersection of poetry, music, and spiritual longing. Miller explains this blending in his memoir *Fathering Words* when he writes, "Yes, Trane was going where I wanted to go: the spiritual development in his last years, the pursuit of music as a way of talking to the Lord, as in "Dear Lord" […] The goal was to reach that point of peacefulness and awareness…the psalm. The sacred song or poem."

Here we sample the blues of art fused with spiritual longing in just a few sparse lines:

> Prayer
>
> dear lord
> may john coltrane
> always pray Dear Lord

Each of these early poems is in dialogue with questions of cultural expression and human rights. Poet Haki Madhubuti stated in an interview, "If an artist, or any person, actually understands the condition of the Black world, it will be a dereliction of duty to not write about that world and expose the injustices that exist in it--injustices imposed upon the weak by white, Black and other cultures." It appears this advice from his mentor resonated with Miller as he uses poetry to probe issues of blackness, of his desire for the world to embrace color. We see this cultural tension in the poem "Howard":

> Between
> the
> vanishing
> Negro

&
the
invisible
black man
I
look
for
change

And while Miller believes such change is possible, the change he envisions is inclusive—the emotions evoked by hardship and celebration are not relegated to one race, one ethnicity, one religion. His poems work to find the tenderness and connective tissue among all men and women in order to further what Martin Luther King, Jr. envisioned as the Beloved Community.

II. *Andromeda* (Chiva Publications, 1974)

*Andromeda* is Miller's first book of poetry, published by Chiva Publications, a small California press. Named after the composition "Andromeda's Suffering" from Alice Coltrane's 1972 album *Lord of Lords*, *Andromeda* was published just two years after Miller graduated from Howard University. Miller's teacher and mentor at Howard, literary critic Stephen Henderson, had encouraged the aspiring poet to continue writing after he graduated. In *Fathering Words*, Miller writes, "The first few years after graduation are when young people should go in search of themselves. They should find their path or what I call their bowl. The journey means confronting one's fears and finding their way out of no way." *Andromeda* represents the beginning of Miller's journey; it is a young man claiming his "bowl" as poet.

In this section you will find the beginnings of a poet who is searching for himself, sensitive to the loneliness and dissatisfaction he both feels within himself and observes in others. *Andromeda's* poems were written with a consciousness of Sufi, Zen, and Islamic teachings. At this time, Miller was influenced by jazz musicians Alice Coltrane, John Coltrane, and Pharoah Sanders. The young poet looked for inspiration in the works of Norman Jordan, Carolyn Rodgers, and Amiri Baraka.

Similar to the *Early Poems*, the *Andromeda* poems are characteristically short, written in lowercase letters, and contain virtually no punctuation.

We see in this section the continuation of many of Miller's early poem themes, notably solitude, sadness, and longing. However, despite the disappointment felt in a world full of injustice, there is an absence of anger and bitterness in his lines.

Miller's poetry was riding a new wave of art that was being produced by African Americans in the wake of the Black Consciousness Movement. He remembers this period as a time when, "Artists were attempting to destroy the negative images that enslaved us and provide us with positive, uplifting ones. So after all this death and destruction, I felt one had to move to the next stage. I saw many of my fellow writers representing a new voice." Miller would add his voice to the conversation. He would acknowledge the darkness, but so too, would he put forth an alternative or allow space for light in his poems. Instead of a militant call for reform, Miller's language is quiet, non-violent. Yet, the message in his words is arresting. Late poet Liam Rector, who directed the Graduate Writing Seminars at Bennington College, called Miller "a Gandhi in our national literary world." Miller's poems speak with the calm of Gandhi, his words flow with the gentle steadfastness of King. These are poems charged with a tender language that simultaneously expresses desperation and longing while searching for change.

> open your eyes
> do not fear the light
> it is the dawn of a new day
> and the end of a long night

> —*from "Daybreak"*

The use of light/dark imagery helps to convey Miller's belief that change can only occur if we embrace the vision of a better world and courageously work to see this "new day" into realization. Such change comes with the adoption of a new language. Words that are assertive, but not violent. Words that foster love, not hate. Words that build a bridge, not tear apart a people. So, using inclusive language becomes especially important here.

Miller uses the word "all" to voice this collective experience. "We are all beggars," the poet asserts in "Beggars." And in "I Lift My Body," the speaker is searching for change found only when he rises from his knees to:

extend
my arms outwards

embracing
ALL

So, even some rules are important to break. "All" warrants capital letters when it represents the embodiment of the change Miller longs to see in the world.

III. *The Land of Smiles and the Land of No Smiles* (Chiva Publications, 1974)

"The opportunity to travel is important for most artists. It offers a chance to step outside of one's culture, to cross the border into new territories, and to network."

"The writer's journey is a discovery of geography as well as spirit... Many of my trips were adventures into darkness. I didn't know what to expect."
                    —E. Ethelbert Miller, excerpts from *Fathering Words*, 2000

In 1974, Miller took a trip to Africa where he attended the Sixth Pan African Congress in Dar Es Salaam, Tanzania. The book-length poem *The Land of Smiles and the Land of No Smiles* was written on the airplane returning home from Tanzania. Miller was following in the footsteps of Langston Hughes, another poet who felt travel was crucial to expanding the artist's vision.

Travel allowed Miller the opportunity to form lasting relationships with people who would inspire his poetry and influence his worldview. In Tanzania, Miller would meet and interview South African poet Dennis Brutus, a major opponent of South African apartheid. Miller would also have the privilege of meeting Tanzania's President Julius Nyerere. Years later when Miller became a father to his second child, he named his son Nyere-Gibran after the "gentle-soul" of President Nyerere and the Lebanese poet Kahlil Gibran. Miller writes in his first memoir that this choice was made in hopes that "the name Nyere would make my son more aware of Africa and Gibran would remind him to always have poetry in his life."

In the poem *The Land of Smiles and the Land of No Smiles,* Miller attempts to show Africa's response to the West and Western imperialism. During a conversation about the book's creation process, he explains to me that the poem utilizes white space on every page to "capture the distance between Africa and what was being defined as the New World."

Miller's trademark themes of sadness and longing are felt in each line. However, the poem works to emphasize a collective despair:

> in the land of no smiles
> every soul is trapped
>
> every soul longs for the
> season of escape

"Escape" comes in the form of creation. The poet must father words to free himself.

> In the land of smiles
> My memory is LYNCHED
>
> It hangs quietly
> dangling
> blown
> by the dry winds
> of the dry
> seasons
>
> waiting for my imagination
> to cut it down
>
> my imagination is coming

Freedom is possible but depends on the writer's ability to imagine a different world. Miller's poem becomes the liberator of memory, the creation of a new reality.

IV. *Migrant Worker* (Washington Writers' Publishing House, 1978)

When *Migrant Worker* was published in 1978 with help from poet and radio personality Grace Cavalieri, Miller had created an atmosphere that was conducive for an emerging poet to thrive. He had become disciplined in the craft of writing; poetry was not just a side interest. He surrounded himself with other poets, flourishing in the creative energy. One of these poets was Ahmos Zu-Bolton. Hailing from Louisiana, Zu-Bolton wrote poems rich with blues and folklore. Miller admired Zu-Bolton's work, so different from his own, and the two developed a strong friendship. Together they edited *Synergy* (the first anthology of D.C. poetry) and *Hoo Doo Magazine,* and ran the African American Resource Center at Howard. It was on a road trip back to Miller's New York stomping grounds with Zu-Bolton that the two met the enamoring poet June Jordan at a book party coordinated by Toni Morrison to celebrate the release of work by Henry Dumas.

Miller felt it was important to support his fellow poets by promoting their work and providing a platform for them to share their poetry with the public. In 1974, four years prior to the publication of *Migrant Worker,* Miller had launched *Ascension,* a poetry reading series that ran for nearly thirty years, beginning at Howard and eventually moving outside to include the greater D.C. area. Zu-Bolton had many connections with established poets and shared these contacts with Miller so that the poetry series could feature published poets alongside D.C.'s up-and-coming writers. Lucille Clifton was the first featured poet Zu-Bolton helped Miller obtain for a reading. Zu-Bolton would also be instrumental in getting the late poets Wanda Coleman and Ai to give readings for the *Ascension* series.

The book title *Migrant Worker* pays homage to Miller's grandfather and other family members who left their home in Barbados to work on the construction of the Panama Canal. There are strains of sorrow and loneliness and questions of human rights in this underscore of displacement and menial work. Where is connection found in such a relocation and cultural shift? In the poem "Bronx Bajans," we see a family striving to maintain its sense of unity despite being geographically uprooted:

> bergen street and franklin avenue
> where everyone was cousin
> aunt and uncle
> where talk was about back home
> and who died
> and who got married
> and who we were

While there are poems like "Noah" and "Joseph" that make use of Christian images and biblical references to depict relationships with women, perhaps most memorable are the poems that were inspired by Zu-Bolton's poetry. The unusually long "Deridder: The Southern Sequence to Southern Spirit" pays tribute to Zu-Bolton's role as poet/ storyteller and conjures up several of the personas found in his poems, as an outgrowth of Miller's road trip down South with Zu-Bolton in 1974. Some of the poem's lines are written like intricate koans:

> in the house of zu
> every child must learn
> to read the mirror of life
> before looking into it

Each stanza is packed with what we would expect in the oral tradition— narratives infused with cultural values and didactic teachings. Miller inserts humor to lighten the heavy-handedness of such moral directives:

> in the last election
> to decide to change the
> deridder law
>
> the god fearing people
> fixed the ballots
> by having dead people
> vote
>
> "dead people don't
> care too much about
> changing things"
> someone said

But the acknowledgment of a needed change and the subsequent search for ways to achieve freedom bring us back to what is at the heart of much of Miller's work. Escape is possible in the hands of the poet.

> both kids always dreamed
> of leaving deridder
>
> their dreams always tried
> to escape the bars of ollie street

ollie street
is two blocks long

with two deadends

In the spirit of Langston Hughes, Miller will "hold fast to dreams."
Refusing to resign to the dead ends in life, Miller's poems offer lines
leading to an alternate path.

## V. *Season of Hunger / Cry of Rain* (Lotus Press, 1982)

Miller's persistence in surrounding himself with literary influences and
befriending other poets would again pay off for his next publication of
*Season of Hunger / Cry of Rain.* At poet May Miller's suggestion, Naomi
Madgett, owner of Lotus Press, signed on Miller and published this
collection. June Jordan would write the introduction, and Miller would
include a short poem dedicated to her. The intensity of emotion captured
in just a few lines is what Miller does best:

tonight I have flashes
of being the streaks of silver
in your hair

And such powerful statements so succinctly written is perhaps the
language of love between poets. Consider Jordan's rationale for why we
keep on loving:

we survive our love
because we go on

loving
—*From "Grand Army Plaza"*

The poems within *Season of Hunger / Cry of Rain* all seem to echo these
questions: where can I find the "flashes" of love, and how do I keep
going on when love has disappeared? In a world with dark chapters of
history, do we search for connection out of necessity and survival, as
suggested in the slave ship metaphor of "Tomorrow":

it
would be better
to be packed
like spoons again
than
to continue to
live among
knives and forks

Does hunger for intimacy find its root in alienation? So many of Miller's poems cry out for rain from spaces of solitude. In "Sand," the poet writes:

loneliness turns men
into sand

the desert
that separates
us
cannot be crossed

And in "Marathon," we feel this separation and long for the touch of another when a morning is described as:

the deadness of sleep alive in this world
the empty parks filled with unloved strangers
buildings gray with solitude

The search for intimacy, the ache of finding oneself sitting alone, the sting of rejection—all are found in this collection. With its book cover art by Mark Montgomery displaying a naked figure on the ground clutching the sides of an enormous bowl, the man holds emptiness and tips his head up to gaze into a mercilessly blazing sun.

Perhaps a poem like "Song for My Lady or Excuse Me McCoy" is the growling protest. A demand for some rain, for love to fill one's bowl. At a 2015 reading at the Library of Congress as part of Black History Month, the audience laughs and claps in places before Miller can finish reading the poem that has become a crowd favorite. The poem is, in part, a complaint against a lover's conditional affections:

i do not need another woman to tell me
that what's hers belongs to the drummer
and what's mine is fine
but it just don't swing
i am tired of telling women
that I am better than bebop
that what I got is the new thing

Miller's wry humor is just one layer—a soft undertone—in a set where the horn peals the notes of a bittersweet loneliness and the piano responds by playing the keys of love yearned for. The poem becomes the vessel that contains this song, often dedicated to those loves the poet has lost.

VI. *Where Are the Love Poems for Dictators?* (Open Hand Publishing, LLC, 1986)

The publication of *Where Are the Love Poems for Dictators?* marks a shift in Miller's career as poet and literary activist. While his work leading up to this book had primarily been influenced by concerns of the Black Arts Movement and domestic issues, now Miller would expand his focus to adopt a more global consciousness. Especially moved by his travels to Cuba and Central America and friendships he forged with writers from El Salvador, Nicaragua, and Chile, Miller was inspired to write poetry that probed issues of oppression and human rights occurring around the world.

In an essay entitled *My Language, My Imagination: The Politics of Poetry,* Miller clarifies that he was "not a political activist who began to write but a writer who was slowly becoming an activist." By this point in his career, though he identified himself first and foremost as poet, he could not ignore the duty he felt all writers must fulfill—to report what you see in the world (both the shadows and light), promote goodness, and envision change. *Where Are the Love Poems for Dictators?* is a collection of poems that responds to these assumed responsibilities of the writer. The book was published by Open Hand Publishing, operated by Anna Johnson. Miller had worked with the company in years prior when he assisted Johnson with the publication of *The Making of Black Revolutionaries* by James Forman, a civil rights activist who played a crucial role in the organization and mobilization of the Student Nonviolent Coordinating Committee. John Cavanagh, director of Washington's progressive multi-issue think tank, the Institute for Policy Studies (IPS), would write the introduction for *Where Are the Love Poems for Dictators?* when the collection was reprinted in 2001. Cavanagh's friendship with Miller began in the early 1980s when the two began working together on the advisory board of the IPS. Miller would later become chair of the board in 2006 and stills holds this position.

In an interview, Cavanagh touches on what makes Miller such a rare and valuable colleague and friend: "A poet chairing the board of a think tank? Miller might be the first. And, he does it brilliantly. He is beloved by our staff and board alike. He is dignified. He is a dapper dresser. He makes me laugh and think in the same sentence. I love this man."

Indeed, so many of Miller's friends and colleagues report similar experiences with the poet who is constantly observing, questioning, and making connections with his relationships and his words. Meaningful relationships with writers such as Ariel Dorfman, Carolyn Forché, and Roberto Vargas would help him find the words to write the poems found on the pages of *Where Are the Love Poems for Dictators?* We see the victims of oppression and faces of quiet desperation in a poem like "Senor Rodriguez":

> we all carry machetes
> the inside of our hands hard like the earth
> we live on
> our shirts hang from our chests like leaves too
> tired to fall

Such a direct account assigns a writer the role of poetic witness, a dramatic position that other poets like Forché utilize in their works. Indeed, Miller incorporates this approach; he creates a persona or mask to write convincingly about injustices he has not personally endured but can imagine viscerally and recount with precise detail. Similar to strategies employed by a method actor, the poet often uses his own relatable experiences as a way to access the emotions of a story he has not lived but is reporting on as if the story has emerged from his own paradigm. Consider these lines from "Nicaragua":

> i will remember you dressing in the morning
> near the window
> i will remember your voice
> and the way the wind carried your song
> into the mountains

These lines may well have been from one of Miller's poems dedicated to a lover lost, capturing the memory of an intimate moment before they parted. What difference is there in the emotion that finds its way into the poet's love song written for a country lost?

The mask Miller wears to write poems outside of his experience is still worn when he returns once again to the U.S. to offer stories that speak of injustices found within our own country's borders. Miller's use of a mask was inspired by writers Ai and Appalachian poet Lee Howard. Memorable in this collection are poems that show the poet's ability to juxtapose childhood innocence with a much darker and disturbing reality. In the poem "Elaine Beckford," a violent crime has occurred, but the speaker's memories of that time paint a very different picture:

> and maybe a few of us like ginger and eddie
> would toss rocks into the water
> take our shoes off
> splash each other and try to scoop
> small fish up with our hands
> our world was perfect
> like sunlight coming through the curtains

So, too, is the young narrator in "Mississippi" displaying a child's inability to understand a world that holds both light and darkness:

> death surrounds itself with the living
> i watch them take the body from the house
> i'm a young kid maybe five years old
> the whole thing makes no sense to me

Miller's poems, whether written from the point of view of an Argentinian political prisoner or child living in the deep south of Mississippi, challenge us to question how people with the potential for such goodness can commit such horrific acts. He asks us to sit with these questions and, in our discomfort, be moved to say no more. This is the goal of poet and literary activist—to write the truth, and in so doing, call for change.

It should come as no surprise that Gwendolyn Brooks endorsed the poems found in *Where Are the Love Poems for Dictators?*, calling Miller "one of the most significant and influential poets of our time."

## VII. *First Light* (Black Classic Press, 1994)

This collection of poetry celebrates the start of Miller's publishing partnership with Paul Coates and Black Classic Press. Founded in 1978, the mission of Black Classic Press is to publish writings "by and about people of African descent" to ensure that there is a literary representation of the Black experience. Coates would publish Miller's next poetry collection *Whispers, Secrets and Promises* and reprint his memoir *Fathering Words*.

There is a lapse of eight years between *Where Are the Love Poems for Dictators?* and *First Light*, a collection of new and selected poems, where punctuation is more frequently employed than in Miller's past collections. Question marks often visit the lines of these poems that call for introspection, and periods are likely to take their position at the ends of final stanzas.

While the poet's last published collection is concentrated largely outside the U.S. to consider world injustices, this new collection is almost a homecoming of sorts, a look back at the writer's beginnings and issues of family and identity. Looking outside at the overwhelming problems of the world might prompt one to return to the self for evaluation; are our affairs in order at home? Many of the autobiographical poems included in *First Light* would be echoed in prose when Miller writes his first memoir in 2000. Even the term "first light" would hold significance in the memoir; Miller connects these two words with the Bible's beginning, or Genesis, as he writes about the genesis of his own family. The poet writes about his father after Egberto Miller learns he will have his first child, "In the dark Egberto reads and dreams about the baby boy to be born, his son and first light." This first light would be named Richard, the poet's older brother. Miller admired Richard, a gentle-spirited, bright soul who left the family in South Bronx to become a Trappist monk and returned a year later after being pressured by his mother to come back home. Many poems in this collection are a tribute to Richard and the soft, spiritual footsteps he left behind when he died unexpectedly in his sleep from a heart attack.

> to give your son
> up to the lord is one thing
> to receive him back is another
> i would not have been surprised

if my father had lived the
rest of his life on his knees
i knew how grateful he was

faith is the meaning of love
between men

—*From "Faith: My Brother Richard Returns Home From the Monastery"*

Haki Madhubuti, who had known Miller at the beginning of his journey and given him encouragement along the way, contacted the publisher to ask if he could write an introduction for the collection. Calling Miller a "word-musician," Madhubuti applauds the poet for the musicality of his language used to breathe light into the story of each of his poems.

These poems tell stories of love, grief, determination, hope. They examine even the most mundane of our daily comings and goings, or what writer Edward P. Jones calls our "days with their blocks of time." But as readers, we see ourselves in these routines. We find small moments of extraordinary in the ordinary, such as the details recorded in the title poem:

it is a few hours before first light
today is mother's day
there is unfinished work on my desk
a few unpaid bills
i have been reading raymond carver
how does a man give birth to a poem?

What is left "unfinished" for a man? For a poet? At the publication of *First Light*, Miller is forty-four years old, just two years past the age his beloved brother Richard had been when he passed away. What matters of the heart still need attention? Loss brings a sense of awareness about our own mortality, the frailty of our lives. While working on this collection, Miller thinks about two men he had lost: his brother and his father.

And he must have been thinking about enduring. In "Survival Poem," dedicated to June Jordan, after experiencing a California earthquake, he writes:

the distance between us
a slight tremor
our love holding up
against the odds

How does one survive against the odds? The poet overcomes by offering poems that stretch out their arms and say here I am. Miller's words are honest, unapologetic. And it is his willingness to show vulnerability that ultimately claims redemption.

VIII. **Whispers, Secrets and Promises** (Black Classic Press, 1998)

Miller begins this 1998 collection with a quote from Emerson—"I have heard that after thirty a man wakes up sad every morning." When Miller writes to me later, he gives me his own interpretation of Emerson's words: "Well, I'm over sixty—so I must be twice as sad. So often I feel that way every day."

The sadness carried on the backs of these poems is deeply felt. Even the back cover with a blurb written by Miller's friend, poet Reetika Vazirani, who took her life in 2003, whispers loss. And inside the pages we hear these melancholy whispers in a poem like "Chalk":

there were streets in the city where there were no
trees or grass or growing things. only a white dust
like chalk, a film, a layer of death covering the
blackness of my flesh and memories of who
we were and what we had become.

The environment mirrors the melancholy in these poems, where no trees or grass grow, or in "I've Been Waiting for a Letter from You," where rain adds its own song of tears:

The sky is dark and rain is coming down
I close my window and pull down the shade
The bed in my room cries itself to sleep

And yet Miller's poetry makes its familiar shift to reaching for love and finding comfort. Distinguished historian Douglas Brinkley, who writes the book's introduction, observes, "More than anything else *Whispers, Secrets and Promises* is about surviving the various storms of life. But rain brings growth, and Miller has the gift of pointing that out, offering hope through lost love in moments of personal despair."

We are allowed to look in on those small, daily exchanges of affection, seen in the poem "When We Are Alone" where a father plays with his children at bedtime:

> It is dark and they cannot
> see. I feel their small bodies
> against mine. A foot pushes into
> the center of my chest. I tickle
> it and it moves away to join a
> silly laugh.

And we are offered moments of profound introspection, when the father reflects:

> The stories begin
> when we are alone and afraid
> of the dark. We need the stories
> to hold us. We need the words to
> keep us warm.

Words become the source of solace, the place where we catch our breath after the rain has fallen. A 2014 post by Miller in his blog *E Notes* would echo the poet's belief that our words and stories sustain us. He shares a few passionate convictions: "…poets always give birth to new words and may these words keep our children safe. Without new words our stories will be an endless cry. Yes, we need the stories to keep us warm. We need the dreams for when we wake."

We seek out the poem when we need healing, but we also need poems that sing our joy. And so the collection also includes poems that hold our dreams. For Miller, this means poems that celebrate what speaks to his heart—jazz, sports (especially baseball), visual arts, and relationships. All good poems to recite when one is walking home and it starts to rain again.

IX. *Buddha Weeping in Winter* (Red Dragonfly Press, 2001)

A year prior to the publication of this collection, poet Quincy Troupe published the title poem "Buddha Weeping in Winter" in Code magazine. Red Dragonfly Press signed on Miller to do a limited edition of a larger body of work that would include the title poem and other pieces that explored Buddhist philosophy and spiritual transcendence. No other collection of Miller's captures spiritual longing quite as extensively and eloquently as *Buddha Weeping in Winter.*

Korean poet and translator Don Mee Choi heavily influenced the writing of the poems in this collection. Choi's support had been instrumental in the creation of Miller's memoir *Fathering Words*, and now she lent her knowledge of Buddhism and spiritual advice to her friend. Many of the poems in *Buddha Weeping in Winter* were found in letters Miller wrote to Choi during several years of correspondence. Choi wrote the introduction for the collection, in which she shared an intimate observation of her friend: "He often let his chin fall into his hands, then withdrew into silence. These silent moments spoke to me of the pain in his heart and his deep longing for a bowl."

This ache to find a bowl is continually present in Miller's work, and we see this quest as one of the paramount concerns in the collection. In "Devotion," the minimal words and meditative tone read like a soft prayer:

> I bow
> my head
> and drink
> from your
> bowl

There is surrender in the simple beauty of these lines, a language offered up that gives control over to someone or something with greater power than we have alone. Indeed, these poems suggest there is something more for us than the temporary world and its broken promises.

Is it possible to live in this imperfect world and still extend love to each other? In "Dear Flower Wife," the speaker concedes our environment encourages the hurt we too often bestow on one another:

> if the winds of my heart cause pain
> it is because of this earth walk

I think once again of Choi's descriptions of Miller and the "pain in his heart" that she heard in the silences shared with the poet. In quiet moments I have seen this sadness, too. Reading through old papers at the Gelman archives, I watched Miller's countenance fall, the light fade from his eyes. He was revisiting old poems he had written to dear friends who were now gone. I sat with him, listening to him talk of friends and lovers who died of AIDs or cancer, or were victims of shootings, or took their own lives. If he held a bowl then, it would have overflowed with sorrow.

But these moments are rare as Miller lets few people see the depths of his blues, and when he does, it is a fleeting moment. He quickly catches himself, smiles, makes a joke to change the mood. "It's not his way," Miller's first wife Michelle Blandburg tells me in a phone interview. She first met Miller nearly forty-five years ago when he offered to show her where the campus bookstore was located. Blandburg goes on to explain that Miller wore what she calls a "masked melancholy" even when he was a young college student—"He doesn't tell his problems, he helps everyone else. He thinks he should not share his problems. His job is to fix."

Before we hang up, I ask Blandburg what I have wanted to ask Miller:

"Do you think the poem holds his sadness?"

Blandburg agrees that poetry is cathartic for Miller. Later, I think about poetry and its potential to soothe and perhaps even heal. I wonder about the repressed emotions of a sensitive poet when I read the title poem of this collection. Miller describes the "endless whiteness" of winter as:

> snow falling on prayers
> covering the path
> made by your
> footprints

And aches for what is lost to be restored:

> i wait for spring
> and the return of love

It is a waiting period of solitude. Is finding a spiritual path the answer? Is writing poems enough to fill this void? Perhaps Miller needs both; a path will give some direction, a poem will serve as vessel for his pain. For how can he burden a friend with his sorrow, risk breaking their back with the weight of his despair?

But a poem cannot break.

X. *How We Sleep on the Nights We Don't Make Love* (Curbstone Books, 2004)

This is the book closest to my heart, for it was at a reading of *How We Sleep on the Nights We Don't Make Love* that I first met Miller. In 2007, he was the Visiting Poet at Marymount University, where I was finishing an undergraduate degree in English. I had attended his reading and was transfixed by the way Miller's poetry moved through the air of the room and found its way into the hearts of the audience. After the reading, Miller sat at a table and graciously signed books and talked with the students and faculty. When it was my turn, I had shyly made my way up to the table, handed him my book, and mustered up the courage to tell him I was an aspiring poet. He looked up at me and smiled, wrote down his email, and told me to send him a few of my poems, and he would give me some feedback. It was the start of a friendship that would become a working relationship as well when I helped edit his second memoir *The Fifth Inning* in 2008. Later, he would sit on my graduate thesis panel in 2013. When Miller asked me to enter into a year-long project as editor for this book of his collected poems in 2014, I quickly responded, "yes."

This section from *How We Sleep on the Nights We Don't Make Love* offers a mix of poems that speak of desire, play with words, examine violence, and experiment with the narrative voice. Here we see Miller begin to abandon his use of only lowercase letters. The collection is notable for its inclusion of two sets of "series" poems—the "Omar" poems and the "Rebecca" poems. These series poems masterfully use the persona approach to create characters who encounter challenges and demonstrate admirable resilience.

In the "Omar" poems, we watch the unfolding of a friendship between two young boys. At first glance, the poem's narrator, a street-wise African-American boy, appears to have nothing in common with Omar, his Islamic schoolmate. However, the two build a strong bond out of mutual respect. In "Sister Sheba, Omar & Me," we become aware that not everyone is so quick to embrace cultural diversity. Many of the adults who take on a teaching role in the "Omar" poems could stand to learn a lesson on tolerance from the boys:

> Omar takes off his shoes
> whenever he comes to see me
> just like in the mosque he's always talking
> about and I ain't seen because my momma
> say *boy you was a problem in my womb and*
> *so I don't need you around no strange influences*

Capturing the child language in the "Omar" poems proved itself difficult at first. Miller's earliest attempts are two "Omar" poems in *Whispers, Secrets and Promises*, but he is critical of these first pieces. He paraphrases the words of jazz saxophonist and composer Charlie Parker: "I can hear the new music. I just can't play it yet." Miller explains he could only hear the music when he wrote his first two "Omar" poems. It was not until he wrote the "Omar" poems included in *How We Sleep on the Nights We Don't Make Love* that he could hear *and* play the language.

While capturing the right language is essential in a persona poem, it is equally important to capture the sound of the speaker's heart. Miller writes the heartbeat into his poems, and we hear its rhythmic beating as love and joy are sought after, even in the presence of difficult obstacles. We hear this beating particularly in the "Rebecca" poems. First appearing in the *First Light* collection, the "Rebecca" poems trace the life of a woman who has undergone a mastectomy and continues to battle breast cancer. In "Rebecca Lets Down Her Hair," the title character, who has already lost one of her breasts, must now lose one more representation of her womanhood and identity:

> I am a victim
> of my own war
> as I stand in the
> shower watching
> my hair fall and
> swim

In spite of her grievances, Rebecca searches for connection in the arms of a lover in "Rebecca Hides Her Scar." She longs for intimacy—even if it is found in an affair—to help her believe love, like the body, can be restored.

When my lover touches me
it feels like the first time...
My body is new again.
Nothing is broken.
Nothing needs repair.

The "Rebecca" poems would hold new meaning when Miller learned his beloved friend June Jordan was diagnosed with breast cancer. Jordan would lose her battle to breast cancer in 2002. The "Rebecca" poems endure and bear witness for those we have lost and those still fighting to free their lives from cancer's grip.

XI. *The Ear Is an Organ Made for Love* (online publishing, 2010) http:// www.eethelbertmiller.com/TheEarIsAnOrgan.html

This collection was self-published by Miller and shows the poet's willingness to play and experiment with his craft. In *The Ear Is an Organ Made for Love*, Miller embraces modes of erasure, the surreal, and ekphrasis in these poems. Much of the work included in this section originates from email correspondence. "The 10 Race Koans" is a poem inspired by an idea Miller set forth in an email to his friend, respected scholar and author Charles Johnson. No doubt his poem is a gift of friendship extended to Johnson, a practicing Buddhist aware of the koan's meditative and cathartic powers. In "Race Koan #6," the poet asks:

A blind black man
boards a bus.
What do you notice first
his blindness or blackness?

It is the type of question Miller would likely ask Johnson years later when the two collaborated on a year-long interview project that would culminate in the publication of *The Words and Wisdom of Charles Johnson.* I email Johnson to ask my own questions:

"Would you like to make any specific comments on Miller's work? (Such as aesthetic concerns, themes, historical issues, etc.) How has his work impacted/inspired you?"

*xliv*

Johnson responds by telling me in his most recently published book he wrote a short story that references Miller's title poem, "The Ear Is an Organ Made for Love." Johnson explains his reason for using Miller's poem: "That's a poem I admire, and I think it captures Ethelbert's love of language (as a poet), and how language is a vital means for expressing consciousness (and the human heart) in the social world."

One look at the opening lines of "The Ear Is an Organ Made for Love" and we see what Johnson means when he references Miller's delight in language. Only here, we see the poet's disheartened response to what can be viewed as the decay of our language.

> It was the language that left us first,
> The Great Migration of words. When people
> spoke they punched each other in the mouth.
> There was no vocabulary for love…

This title poem was inspired by a visit from Miller's friend Me-K from South Korea. The two had spent time together touring Washington, D.C. and were shocked to hear the way words were being abused. In a 2011 *Words Without Borders* interview, Miller recounted his impressions of that visit, "Riding around the city together we listened to the voices of people passing us. Many of their conversations were filled with profanity and what I defined as ugliness. So sad to 'hear' our young people losing their tongues. Where is the new music that will save our ears? Where are the conversations of hope?"

Without words, we find ourselves in a dystopia where our hearts have lost the ability to communicate. Miller has spent his entire career clinging to a vocabulary that finds its origins in an elevated language of love and respect. His poems do not throw around expletives meant only for shock value, nor does he exploit language by using offensive slang that is too often heard in casual conversation. Instead, Miller's poems often grow out of exchanges with friends and display a language of refinement and beauty. He seems to be nostalgic for a different time when etiquette and grooming spoke to who you were, and the words you chose to say to others were a reflection of your character. In "So This Is What the Living Do," Miller remembers a different time when:

> I once believed in love the way I believed in beauty;
> The living with dignity, style and grace.
> I thought my shoes always needed to be polished
> Whenever I left the house.

I think Miller still believes in love and beauty. I think the poet is not ready to give up on dignity, style, and grace. In all the years of our friendship, he has always "polished his shoes." Dressed to the nines, Miller meets me at a coffee shop in his Sunday best. And he has always exhibited the most genteel of manners, helping me adjust my scarf before walking to the metro station in the falling snow to catch a train home.

Miller's poems are as dignified and carefully crafted as their creator. His poems privilege love and language, and the love of language. One of his most popular poems in this collection is "Divine Love." The poem's source can be found in email exchanges between Miller and writer Elizabeth Alexander but would gain crowd appeal when Miller wrote a longer version to present as a wedding gift to his friend writer Alexs Pate and Soo Jin. Such long, elegant lines demonstrate Miller's commitment to the belief that even today, love and beauty are very much present and obtainable:

> I wish I had loved you many years ago.
> I would have loved you like Ellington loved jazz and Bearden loved scissors.
> I would have loved you like Langston loved Harlem and the blues loved Muddy Waters.
> ...
> I would have loved you like Louis loved boxing and Mahalia loved to sing.
> I would have loved you like Carver loved peanuts and Wheatley loved poems.

## XII. *Falta De Ar* (Medula, 2014)

*Falta De Ar* (*The Shortness of Breath*) is a small collection of Miller's poetry dedicated to his friend Beverly Hunt, who continues to battle cancer. The book was published by Medula, a small press run by Portuguese writer and editor Manuel A. Domingos. Around 2010, Domingos had translated and published a few of Miller's poems in a magazine he was editing. Domingos remembered this successful collaboration when he decided to produce a small line of poetry books; he wanted Miller to be among the select few whose work he would publish.

This was not the first time Miller's work was part of a translation project. In 2009, some of his previously published poems were translated into Arabic and published in a collection called *At Night, We Are All Black Poets*, as part of the Abu Dhabi Authority for Culture and Heritage's KALIMA project. Miller described what he saw as the end product of this translation project—his poems had been given "a new wardrobe." In a 2009 *Middle East Online* article, the poet explained the value of translation, "It's a further example of the construction of cultural bridges between people and nations… We live in a world with too many borders. A good poem offers a window into another experience. When words touch the heart everything is possible."

*Falta De Ar* is another good example of translation used to build a "cultural bridge." For this collection, Miller chose shorter pieces for inclusion that he felt would be conducive for translation and easily understood. Yet, despite their short length, these poems hold powerful punches. Consider a poem like "Tubman," inspired by editor Kwame Dawes' challenge for writers to create ekphrastic poetry based on artwork by Romare Bearden. In "Tubman," form embraces subject; we can visualize the small woman (Harriet Tubman was a petite five feet) with larger than life strength:

> Short woman with a gun
> Leading me through the woods
> Footprints left beside rivers

There are also poems that carry a beautiful gentleness. In "I Fall in Love Too Easily," the confession of the title leads into a poem dedicated to Maria Otero. The poet croons:

> Like Miles you lean into me
> Play the center of my back
> With your fingers

These lines, rich with music, are a token of friendship to Otero who co-founded the Humanities Council of Washington, D.C. with Miller. So many poems that appear in Miller's collections are written for or about his friends.

There is also a ubiquitous wisdom found in the poems of *Falta De Ar*. Miller comments to me that some of these poems "come close to being aphorisms…This is something I've been doing more of—and might be a result of blogging and attempting to be profound now and then." I imagine he is smiling and has a light in his eyes when he writes this.

When I revisit his comment, it is nighttime. I think about how we both get little sleep. What keeps Miller awake? Does he write to the darkened sky? Does he think about his fallen friends? Does he search the glow of stars for June and Reetika? For Richard and his father?
In the darkness, I read Miller's poem, "Life":

> There is a ladder in the room
> that goes nowhere

And then I turn to "Alone":

> No moon tonight
> Empty bed
> Pillow on the floor

Actually, he is "profound" quite often.

The next day I send Miller an email. I tell him: "I think aphorisms find their way into your work now more than before largely because you have more 'wear' in the world. When we are young (or when we are simply less experienced writers), using aphorisms may seem too heavy or overly confident. Sure, aphoristic writing is succinct and, at first glance, unassuming, but the words are loaded with such power. A seasoned writer knows better how to use this power without coming across cliché or arrogant; his readers trust the authority in his voice and are more open to embracing the larger truths he is addressing." We can trust Miller's voice and welcome the wisdom each of his poems holds.

XIII. *50 Love Poems to a Friend* (personal collections, 2015)

The poems in this section are important in part because of the reason they were written. A few years ago Miller learned his dear friend Beverly Hunt had been diagnosed with breast cancer. The friendship of over thirty years that Miller shares with Hunt began when she was a student at Howard University and wrote an article on Miller for a journalism class assignment. Hunt remembers the students were asked to write about someone on campus, so she went to her journalism professor after class for suggestions. She explained to her professor she wanted to cover someone "meaningful." The professor suggested Ethelbert Miller.

In the early years of their friendship, Hunt spent a lot of time at Howard's African American Resource Center where Miller was the director. She attended poetry readings in the *Ascension* series which Miller ran. And she was the recipient of Miller's encouragement and generous support as she began her writing career.

Miller maintained his support when Hunt changed careers to go into public relations. But when Hunt revealed to her friend she had an aggressive form of breast cancer and was uncertain she would survive, the poet rallied in the most beautiful act of friendship. "Ethelbert went into overdrive," Hunt writes to me in a letter. Miller began "doing everything he could to communicate how much I meant to him and how he was rooting for me. He even wrote a book of 50 poems for me. That kind of special care allowed me to acknowledge and be in wonder of the lifelong unconditional love that our friendship has grown into."

The book of fifty poems Hunt mentions is what Miller calls "*50 Love Poems to a Friend.*" The first poem is simply titled #50, the age of Hunt when Miller began to write these love poems to his friend. The collection goes to #100, each poem representing one more year that Hunt will reach; so certain is the poet that Hunt will win her battle against cancer. Miller shares with me his thoughts on the creation of the collection: "These are poems similar to sketches. They were an outgrowth of things Beverly said or did. Because she was fighting cancer I wanted the poems to be uplifting. I wanted them to renew and strengthen our friendship."

The poems in this collection, like so much of Miller's work, take risks by exposing a vulnerability in their lines, such as the soul-bearing lines of poem #97:

> What grows green
> are my dreams of you. The
> red nights of passion and
> the fruit of words.
> Come hold the ash of me.
> The black of me now.

Miller lets longing wash over his lines, but he is also careful to instruct the reader to courageously search for love and believe in the heart's potential. Poem #78 reads like a soft embrace:

> The heart is a small
> room. Too often we
> fail to open the window
> and let love in.

I imagine it is easier to "let love in" when you have a friend like Miller who will write you a sky of sunshine when you stand in the dark.

XIV. *New Poems* (personal collections, magazine publications, circa 2012-present)

Similar to the *Early Poems* section, the *New Poems* hold a special magic simply because the poems here have never been published in a book collection. Many of these new poems have never been seen before. Most of us can remember a time when we were a child waiting for the toy store to stock that newest toy we have heard about. For me, it was waiting on a shipment of Cabbage Patch® dolls that boasted "corn silk" hair instead of the old, unrealistic hair made out of yarn. When I finally brought my new doll home and carefully removed her out of her box with its transparent plastic front, I could barely contain my joy. Holding her to me, I had that delightful knowledge that I was one of the first to have this new doll. My friends would want to come over and see her, feel her new hair, and then beg their parents for an advance in their allowances so that they, too, could have a doll just like her. But this doll was mine. And these poems are yours. They are new, fresh out of their package. They don't have notes written between their lines, their pages aren't dog-eared, your friends have not read them yet. They are written for you. These new poems will certainly express the sadness and isolation that Miller's work is known for:

> One slip and the sky
> cracks like bone.
> Nothing heals after
> death. Snow falling
> is the white you
> remember. Loneliness
> becomes the shadow

to growing old. Where
is the resting place
for black?

> —*from "Falling"*

You will still see injustice banging its fist in this section of new poems,
like in *"My Lebanon, My Love"*:

> Please tell me someone overslept
> and a bomb did not explode today.

And Miller will still ask us to restore the beauty of our language. In
a 2010 television interview with news anchor Wendy Rieger, the poet
shared his view on the degradation of our words: "We have really
misused our language. We've damaged it. We've destroyed parts of it...
the language is very muscular. There's hitting, there's punching." With
such language, Miller asks, "How can you embrace someone?"

> Maybe the sickness in the air
> comes from the words we speak.
>
> Press your tears against my eyes
> so that I might see you.

> —*from "Who Said Love Is Blind?"*

In a world where language can be aggressive and abrasive, it becomes
crucial for Miller to offer us poems that renew our faith in love:

> Repair your heart
> before you love.
>
> Touch another person
> with hands that whisper

> —*from "Fix Something That Is Broken"*

Finally, Miller will offer us poems like "If My Blackness Turns to Fruit,"
that will help us believe in transformation and grace:

> Look behind your prison walls.
> Count the black seeds behind bars,

the cells where nothing blooms.
Can hope flower from despair?
Yes, America, my love,
resistance comes and then the rain.

As my work as editor of *The Collected Poems of E. Ethelbert Miller* comes to an end, I think back to a poem I selected for the *Early Poems*—"In Celebration of New Days."

i embrace
the light of the sun
which shines
for the first time

i laugh
i dance
i sing

i celebrate your coming

and
the
coming
of new days

Sadness rushes through me; goodbyes are never easy. And yet, I feel like this is a beginning. And I celebrate the coming of a new day. Will Miller be pitching, or hitting, or catching?

No matter, this is a new game featuring Miller, a poet and friend I love dearly. I'll stand in line to get my game ticket.

I'm praying he'll play extra innings.

—Kirsten Porter
Professor of Literature and Creative Writing
Marymount University

*I.*
*Early Poems*

From the Moon

from the moon
I can see Africa

  (and there is blackness
          between us)

distant
yet closer than the sun

Africa
blows away white clouds

Howard

Between
the
vanishing
Negro
&
the
invisible
black man

I
look
for
change

Winnie

this time the fire did not reach my heart
when the cameras and reporters came
i had already picked through the rubble
i found a wedding gift
pictures of our children
all lying in the ashes
the earth they call south africa
the land i love but cannot own


nelson
tonight

i no longer wait for your release
i no longer wait for the rumor or the promise
i have accepted the loneliness of courage
i have accepted the loneliness of struggle
even when my own people come to burn my home
i will open my arms in welcome
for my love extends to them also
i will forgive them just as africa must forgive
me if ever i stop and say i cannot go on


my dear
nelson

what does it matter if we lose this life
i dream of a tomorrow without funerals
even as your hair turns gray
when you smile i am reminded of that morning
after our marriage
when you promised me a free south africa
and i knew i would love you until death

A Poem for Today—Only Today

there is fever in this land
a sun burning underground and above
a thousand red scars across a sky
filled with sickness

we feel the weakness in our dreams
at night our bodies sleep in blackness
our souls lie awake panting
like the tongues of dogs

we are still a people with masters

## Walter Rodney

after rodney's death
we tried to breathe the air but couldn't
something human in us was lost
hearts placed in chains
we felt the bomb explode in our blood
saw the coming of funerals & ghosts

## Note to Columbus

This land
is not
what you think
it is

this place
is not where
you want to be

turn back
before America
drags you
ashore

Reservations

relationships
are
treaties

we are
all Indians

My Mother Thru the Eyes of My Sister and Myself

when we grew taller
than she was
we would look over
the top of her head
and spot gray
growing among her hairs
and when we attempted
to pick and pull them
out
she would shoo us away
saying that if you
pulled one two would
come back
and grow in its place
and as we grew taller
and one day grew no more
her entire head turned
the color of snowclouds
and we blamed ourselves
for not listening
for pulling out
the gray hairs
while she slept

Grandma

old
she sits
next to
her front
door

sitting
with the
sun
going
down

hands in lap
dressed
in a paisley
dress

an old scarf
around her
head
and woolen
socks around
her feet

old
yet still
a lady
with
womanly
warmth

she's
warm
even after
the sun
sets

Old Men

they spend their last
days picking up newspapers
and cutting grass

the healthy ones
still move furniture

their bodies still sweat

water
ripples
through
the wrinkles
in their
foreheads

sometimes
they will say a few
words when you pass

many times
they just bow their
heads
and stare quietly at
the ground

Every Morning

every morning
when everyone is rushing
to work

aging black faces
can be seen
standing in doorways

or

peeking out onto
streets from behind
torn curtains

and

card board
windows

from cars and buses
these faces appear
somewhat ghostly
and unreal

almost like

sketches of men

Washington D.C. in Spring
        (1974)

a strange quietness
can be smelled and touched

dust bites its way into
the skin of survivors

gone are homes
and all things known as shelters

everywhere around buildings
have been torn down

we alone still stand

standing on the same corners
with nothing behind our backs

we alone still stand

Bo Willie

sometimes
when he thinks
he knows where
he's goin
he be followin
a lost map

My Friend Bo Willie Was a Born Poet

my friend
bo willie
was a born poet

born in a black box
in the small town of
poplarville mississippi
a place that
is ten times larger than
deridder louisiana
and twenty times smaller
than wheaton maryland

here
at the age of 13
bo willie
was given hoo-doo sense
by old mama easta
this helped him in dealing
with the nonsense
of white folks

colored people
claimed that bo willie
could undress a woman
with a poem

old blind preacher reagan
once caught bo willie
preaching naked to his
congregation

called his sermon
the poetry of orgasm

said bo willie
would remain a sinner
if he let women keep his pen

Fightin Man

trouble be comin
me and bo willie
we outnumbered
but we here fightin it all

can't say i take to wounds
never did
never will

bo be checkin the time
eye catchin shadows
he good at it
better than most

drivin outside galveston
headin for the coast

he
tell me
here jack johnson
punched his way out of a woman's womb
bobbed and weaved his way to glory

bo
say he gonna do the same
be a hero
a fightin man

i think he crazy but bo

he older than me
his shadow still young
he drivin
with sun up in his eyes

outside galveston
he enters the ring
hittin 95

i tell bo to go slow

    watch curves

   lean against the ropes

but bo be headin for glory
jack johnson till he die

Legend

"the graveyard
where blackjack
sleeps
lies beneath the
pillow of this earth
under the clouded
skies of legends"
  —ethelbert

I
legend says
that the poet zu
was the first to
hear of blackjack's
death
mama easta came to
him in a dream
spelled blackjack's
name backwards
across his forehead
in blood taken
from malcolm's wounds

II
legend says
that the poet zu
arrived in dc
out of nowhere
talkin about blackjack
bo willie said it was
almost like master fard
bringin silks to detroit

III
legend says
blackjack and zu
began a whole religion
of poetry

out of silversprings
they came
bringing the quickverse
of blacklightning

kids raced down georgia avenue
chasing after it
called it the folklore of the
future
said it was the best creation
since the 45

said the poetry had more soul
than soul music

a howard professor
tried to analyze it
and had to give up
before he started

decided to simply call it
a ufo

Prayer

dear lord
may john coltrane
always pray Dear Lord

How Do Poets Die?

how do poets die?
is it with bleeding hearts
open mouths and silent rooms?

how do poets die?

do they die in their youth
with the poems unpublished
and words never read
or do they die unknown from
pain and age?

how do poets die?

do they kill one another for
the love of art?

hands on each other's throats
cutting into souls and hearts

how do poets die?

is it with the birth of
success and the applause of
crowds?

how do poets die?

is it always a plane or car
crash which takes their lives?

how do poets die?

death writes a poem for every man
and every man asks why?

so I ask myself again and again

how do poets die?

## Lone Journey into Midnight

hands no longer
compose music
on my flesh at night
my bed is a coffin
making a midnight
journey to a final
resting place
past tombstones
and dying floral
wreaths I wander
in my sleep
straining my ears
in search of the
sounds of a new
touch

Columbia Station
*for J. Gaillard*

columbia station
before the renovations and your death
we came to share moments
now so precious as lost jewels
what i wear is your absence
death a wool sweater covering my chest in summer
witness the loving of colors and sounds
the city dancing and strutting down columbia road
my head rests heavy in one hand
at a small table i sit
left with a half bottle of beer
overhearing conversations
amazed and frightened by how fragile they are
each one could be ended by a bullet
columbia station
another monument
here i will speak a silent language when i think of you
you were beyond words
as much as you are beyond life now
who will ever forget the pecan pie lady
the slender slice of sweet womanhood
who slipped through fingers
leaving them sticky with the taste for more

Two Poems for Janet G.
*for Janet Gaillard,*
*killed on September 18, 1977*

I.

the pain
from your death
gives me headaches
the bullet
through
your head
lives in me

II.

september
still warm
you draw
me winter
in still life
(your own)

U.F.O.


the love

you give is strange

so strange

that it seems different

from what I've been seeing

around me

your love is wings

and it can make me fly

people say my nose is

wide open but I say

it never did close anyhow

and besides you smell so

good even my ears be smelling

and my eyes can identify your

scent no matter

how far away you be

from me

Joyce

color her amber
the color of fallen leaves in fall
gather her in your arms
or let the wind take her
when it calls

G.A.

georgia towns
the size of postcards

i want to mail them
back to someone

Listening for the Strayhorn
            *for Gail*

I must dedicate music to you
in my dreams tonight

(the sounds of our first
      meeting should be heard
            again)

the beauty of the ear
is that it cannot help
but listen

## Unpaved Roads

my hands
move slowly
across your
body
stumbling
along
the unpaved
roads
of previous
lovers

For Thulani

girl
what you do is your business
who you love or who you want to love
does not set the sun in my life
there are enough miracles for everyone

girl
i wish you happiness
like a nice home in the country
good playgrounds & schools for your kids
i hope they even learn a second language
translate neruda from english back to spanish

girl
when that man comes along
and tells you that you are like poetry
that in your eyes are all the things he ever imagined
ever wanted
ever needed
never/never mind about what you're gonna wear
just dance with him into forever

girl
don't let no one tell you it ain't time
especially when the fever you have
calls your man doctor & the medicine
is so good you know you can't be well without it

girl
take it and keep it with you
always

Candy

before we undressed
u said your nipples
were like chocolate
and i prayed that they
would melt in my mouth
and not in my hands
cause i would hate to
stop and lick my fingers

Shirley

your hair alabama red
i leave tuskegee
with sunset eyes

Thirst

the dry ground cracking outside
I hear it crying

there are nights when the air cools
and I think of you

thirst holding me back

## Grand Army Plaza
*for June*

here
near the entrance to the subway
the underground
we stand in each other's eyes
once lovers
now friends
we have walked the five or six blocks
from your house to
here
where the night is not dark
where the light from the street
shines on the small wet spot
on the head of your dog
who pulls slightly on the leash
you hold
here
with one hand
and it is the other that i think
about shaking before i leave
now that we are friends
and women love women
and men love men
and many of us are alone
despite it all
here
in grand army plaza
i think of soldiers departing
to fight a civil war
to be wounded and to die
i think of a man
and a woman
lovers
now saying farewell
here

i take you in my arms
hatless and out of uniform
like an unlisted man
afraid of going south

Indian Summer
*for June*

dream
the
way
you
appear
at
dusk

long
after
the
morning

gone

East Hampton
  *for June*

i need
to touch the mimosa trees
in the spring
in the morning
behind your house
when i rise
on forgotten days
remembered from my life

## Space Is the Place

love is the last planet in our solar
system. your heart crying like the
rings of saturn. how can we believe
in stars in this darkness? i watch
the sky for your return. inside my
hands nothing but gravity.

Samson
  *for S.T.B.*

the sadness tonight is too heavy for eyes
i cannot sleep
stars fall and i witness the crumbling of heavens
all things holy have been destroyed
i wander in nightmare
the skull of a beast in my hand
i will slay all monsters and give my life
the peace it needs
before a woman gives me love
before i awake to find my head shaven and my
strength gone

In the Early Morning Hours

in the
early
morning
hours

students
plot
revolution
while
listening
to themselves
and talking
to each
other

from
their
walls
playboy
bunnies
smile
their
rewards

In Celebration of New Days

after
clouds

after
rain

after
puddles

after
morning

after
afternoon

i run outside to watch
the earth
dry itself

i embrace
the wind
the smell of grass
the smell of trees

i embrace
the light of the sun
which shines
for the first time

i laugh
i dance
i sing

i celebrate your coming

and
the
coming
of new days

*II.*
*Andromeda*

Daybreak

open your eyes
do not fear the light

it is the dawn of a new day
and the end of a long night

The Kneelers

the old
prayers
answered

　　we kneelers
　　now stand
　　and walk away

the new
prayers
will
bring us
back

Within Music

within music
there is silence

within love
there is loneliness

Untitled

we
waited
so long
to touch

that fingers
dripped
tears

into
palms

Beggars

we are all beggars
when it comes to love

our hands reach out
desperately to the
hands of others

loving words we cast
like nets to trap and
bring us closer

I Have Seen the Many Faces

I have seen the many faces
after the rain
unwashed and unclean
appearing unrecognized
and I have looked upon the
wetness of another day
still troubled by the
dryness of another life
and smiles and stares and
total disregard cling to
my skin and bones and I
walk alone withholding the
pain which living has
inflicted and the eyes of
my face are wet and dripping
and long after the rain my
cheeks are stained and
the man I have just passed
who looked like me
has passed away

There Are Many Worlds

there are many worlds
still unknown and waiting
to be explored

our minds know no boundaries

and our dreams
exist like grains of sand
reflecting the sun's light

from an eternal shore

I Lift My Body

I
lift my body

out of earth's
blackness

and

extend
my arms outwards

embracing

ALL

At the End of the Universe

at the end of the
universe

there are no shadows
of men

only gods witness
the splendor

of what lies beyond

It's Time to Find Direction

it's time
to find
direction

to step
out of
darkness

and step
beyond
blackness

*III.*
*The Land of Smiles and the*
*Land of No Smiles*

The Land of Smiles and the Land of No Smiles

I cross the ocean of skeletons
to a land white with death

above my head the air is heavy

I have trouble taking it in
and letting it out

phallic monuments
rape the skies of my mother

blood falls instead of rain

in the land of no smiles
two legged creatures hide behind
masks of deceit and plot
destruction

I am in the land of no smiles
because History knocked on
my father's door

my father welcomed History as
a guest

until

History took advantage of him

History demanded many things

I WAS TAKEN FROM MY FATHER

BY HISTORY

I WAS TAKEN FROM THE LAND
OF SMILES TO THE LAND OF
NO SMILES

In the land of smiles
beautiful things are many

even the wind that passes
unseen is beautiful

in the land of smiles
my sisters dance
without the fear of
lust attacking them

their hips hypnotize
all things with eyes

in the land of smiles
laughter is the bride
of happiness
and winter does not
wear dark clothes

in the land of smiles
death is a son of life
and not a robber of
dreams

in the land of smiles
there is joy and peace

in the land of no smiles

two legged creatures
are hostile to the warm
darkness

of my skin

I am a prisoner of History
BEATING MY BLACKNESS
against the bars of western
civilization

in the land of no smiles
every soul is trapped

every soul longs for the
season of escape

at the beginning of my
memory are animals and trees

the sweet earth is good
for farming

At the beginning of my
memory

the land of smiles extends
beyond the hands of distance

In the land of smiles
My memory is LYNCHED

It hangs quietly
dangling
blown
by the dry winds
of the dry
seasons

waiting for my imagination
to cut it down

my imagination is coming

my imagination is coming
from the land of smiles

all the things
inside my mind seem crazy
and unreal

my thoughts appear before
my life like mirrors

my imagination looks
back at me

my imagination is a reflection
of the past and the future
beyond the infinity
to come




my imagination is coming

my imagination is coming
from the land of smiles

*IV.*
*Migrant Worker*

Noah
  *for June*

i am noah
in search of a storm
a destruction to dissolve this distance
hear me oh lord
send me a sign
a second flowering
beneath the rain

Joseph

the phone would ring late almost every night.
tired. i would answer it around the fifth ring.
i would hear her voice.

joseph. joseph. joseph did i wake you?

and i would say

no—i'm all right. i'm up. what's wrong?

and her voice soft and sad would cry out about the problems that
she had.

and me—joseph—i would listen.

i can't seem to sleep. the landlord wants me to move
joseph. i know it's because i'm pregnant. he wants to
get rid of me before i have the child. joseph what am
i going to do? i don't have a job. i can't move. i can't
sleep joseph. i'm worried. help me joseph.

and i—joseph would rise late at night. dress.
walk the cold streets to her apartment.

and she would answer the door. her face disturbed
wet. and i would say

mary don't you weep
mary don't you moan.

and would take her in my arms. cause i am joseph.

and she pregnant

from some man i never knew. never saw.
she would talk until the early
morning hours about men. black men.
about how she didn't trust them anymore.
about how a good man was hard to find.
she said she would never get married.
that she would have the baby and raise
it by herself.
and i listening to all this would
break my silence. and tell her that if
she needed any help she could depend on me.

you're a good man joseph—she would always say.
and it would be morning.
and she would fix me tea. and then i would rise to leave.
telling her about a cheap apartment
she could probably afford
a place that accepted children.

and before closing the door
she would ask

     joseph—will you go with me?
     perhaps the landlord will think
     we're married.

and i– joseph would only nod my head.
walk towards the elevator.
turn and say

     i'll see you soon.

outside the morning air despite its cold
would warm me.
and i would head back home. alone.

a slender black man
no longer believing in miracles.
messiahs. or even women.

no longer wishing to be known simply
as the good man

i am joseph. joseph.
a father without a child.

Moses

her body was on fire beneath his.

her hands on his back scratched words
into his flesh. his shoulders were like
tablets. broad and strong.

they loved
until morning
until daylight forced him from her bed.
out the room and door.

hair uncombed.
it stood like horns upon his head.

an old woman passing
was shocked by this presence

frightened by the fire in his eyes.

Jesus

on the day my grandfather died
his daughter the oldest
rushed to his house. there as his
body changed seasons she held
him in her arms, washed his body
with tears. when I was born
i almost died. my mother took me back
to the hospital. i was a blue baby
no one thought would live.
it was a miracle or so they
say.  it was winter and the holiday
season. thanksgiving or christmas
i don't remember.

Deridder: The Southern Sequence to Southern Spirit

on ollie street
in deridder louisiana
13 spirits live in the house of zu

I.
In the house of zu
the bible still works
it runs well even without
batteries

all children born in this house
are taught early to recognize
the ways of the devil

They are constantly reminded
that "god don't like ugly"

in the house of zu
every child must learn
to read the mirror of life
before looking into it

II.
the poet ahmos was
the rebel spirit in the house of zu

he was the spirit that rejected god
and fell up into the hellfires of
the north

he is the spirit old folks say
took up writing because he could not see

III.
in deridder
there are more churches
than there are pews

IV.
russell chew
is the preacher for
the church of the living god

a slender man
he took it upon himself
not to let evil by

V.
when the poet ahmos
came home to deridder
his mother met him at the door

she gave him a strange look
and without a kiss
said in a stranger's voice

"i'll tell you right now son
there ain't gonna be no
curses in my home
make sure when you come in
that you leave dem poems
at the door"

VI.
deridder is a dry town
some folks like it
that way
others are into bootlegging

in the last election
to decide to change the
deridder law

the god fearing people
fixed the ballots
by having dead people
vote

"dead people don't
care too much about
changing things"

someone said

VII.
mrs. clay
lives next door to
russell chew

old
her face seems
no longer to age

her features speak
of indian blood

but her
grandchildren
are the only tribe
she claims

VIII.
people on ollie street
have memories that remember
old things

they can remember the small ahmos
before he picked up his pen
they can remember the young chew
before he carried the cross

both kids always dreamed
of leaving deridder

their dreams always tried
to escape the bars of ollie street

ollie street
is two blocks long

with two deadends

IX.
mrs. clay
once told russell chew
that there was more
to religion than just praying

chew responded by saying

"until folks stop running
away from jesus
it's good to keep them on
their knees"

X.
in deridder
the same things
come and go

each day brings
the same

the bible
is read

before
sunrise

and

after
sunset

The Return of Bo Willie
              *for Ahmos*

blues deep behind his face
this man returns to d.c.
singing spirituals
the tambourine in his hand
a metal disc
a tape recording of his travels

some say they are stranger than life
stranger than nixon's memoirs

this man returning
to d.c.

i meet him at the road's bend
where our friendship keeps turning

the world
light years away
a metal disc...

## Bronx Bajans

we would take the train to brooklyn
leaving the bronx
down through harlem
out to prospect park
bergen street and franklin avenue
where everyone was cousin
aunt and uncle
where talk was about back home
and who died
and who got married
and who we were
we were always reminded
on sundays

Spanish Conversation

in cuba
a dark skin woman asks me
if i'm from angola
i try to explain in the no spanish i know
that i am american

she finds this difficult to believe
at times i do too

Solidarity
*for Roberto Vargas*

when trees bend funny and out of shape
when lightblue skies turn blueblack gray
hungry winds will
knock behind the bellycaves
of coffee colored strangers
and hurricanes will come
and speak no english

## Migrant Worker

a migrant worker          me
i pass push through the crowd
someone hands me a handout a flyer
telling me to either beware
or become involved
i continue to pass push through the crowd
drop the paper to the ground
a foot covers it
then it's gone
me i'm still here

some speaker is speaking through his mike
i can't understand
can't hear
funny i don't even care
cause
the thrill is gone
and i'm just passing through
picking up slogans
humming the songs of last year's harvest

i'm a migrant worker
looking for a home      a job
some cause to believe in
but the thrill is gone

words rain on me
steady and consistent
there has always been clouds
the world is overcast
gone gray     lifeless
there is nothing in this land
that will grow without the nourishment
of blood

that has grown without the nourishment
of blood

i pass push through the crowd
a migrant worker
speaking a language
that has no words
me      i want to yell
join hands demonstrate
free my brothers around the world
free the world around my brothers
but the thrill is gone

a migrant worker
i pass push through the crowd
reach another city
come to this same place
like a hitchhiker
thumbs out on a highway

i don't drive
i don't demonstrate
i don't even believe what folks
be telling me
a migrant worker      i don't even belong here
the guy with the flyers
who is he?      does he know my name?
i don't take nothing from nobody
i don't drive
i don't demonstrate
i barely believe          believe me

i just want to work   earn my pay   make my way
i believe in america more than i believe in myself
me I'm a migrant worker
i've done seen everything
done everything

only reason i'm here is because
the thrill is gone

i don't pick cotton
i don't pick fruit
i  pick winners and losers
and stay away from both

Who Will Call This Day to Prayer
*A poem on the Hanafi Muslim Terrorist Takeover*
*of three D.C. buildings, March 9-11, 1977.*

> Fight in the cause of God
> Those who fight you
> But do not transgress limits;
> For God loveth not transgressors.

THE HOLY QURAN

I.
morning
wednesday
march 9th
this city
wakes and rises
sunlight
calls
this day
to prayer

slowly like a creeping shadow
prepared to darken an afternoon
a small bold band of holy men
plot to hold
to seize control

of this day
wednesday
march 9th

II.
SUDDENLY...in a building
visitors and workers
are forced to move upstairs

herded like cattle
fear branded in their eyes

NOW...the mosque
a sacred place
the true believers show their face

and at the final place and point in time
a third site completes the strange but crooked
line

here a councilman is shot he hits the ground
here a news reporter gets his life cut down
here the mayor is barricaded from the town

while the sun sets to kneel behind the Islamic Center
red blood dripping from revenge
behind its evening veil

as a small food wagon pulls into Scott Circle
with food to feed the ring of hungry newsmen
who watch the starving relatives wailing outside
the B'nai B'rith walls

as the bright lights begin to fill the silent night
that begins to fall

at eleven p.m.
the mystery
the mystery still unfolds

who is a hostage?
who is left?
who are these Hanafi
muslims
who will fight
until the death?

BRING ME THE MURDERERS OF MY BABIES
BRING ME THE KILLERS WHO KILLED THE
ONES I LOVED

who is a hostage?
who is left?
who are these Hanafi
muslims
who will fight
until the death?

WE DO NOT WISH THE MOVIE
MOHAMAD TO BE SEEN
WE DO NOT WISH TO RECEIVE INSULT TO
OUR FAITH AND TO OUR CREED
WE DEMAND THIS MOVIE BE REMOVED
FROM EVERY MOVIE SCREEN

who is a hostage?
who is left?
who are these Hanafi
muslims
who will fight
until the death?

III.
morning
thursday
march 10th

papers proclaim a holy war

ambassadors from the east
Pakistan
Egypt and Iran
are summoned

to plead
to bargain with
the one they
call the crazy man

and who will call this day to prayer
who will put an end to the long nightmare?

IV.
morning
friday
march 11th

the sounds of church bells greet the air

this city
wakes and rises
sunlight
calls
this day
to prayer

but on the floor the blood remains
the hand that held the sword is stained

Untitled

we are all
black poets
at night

Caves

we are cave dwellers
discovering the fire
of each other's love
in darkness
we paint pictures on the walls
of flesh
on the walls of desire
we are cave dwellers
primitive in that we cannot
explain what we feel
we are not writers but lovers
we are cave dwellers
worshippers of the night
erectors of columns
builders of monuments
keepers of rituals
we are cave dwellers
we believe in magic
we circle each other
with song and dance
we return music to the land
we are cave dwellers
beneath moons and suns
the stars speak
loudly of our legends

*V.*
*Season of Hunger / Cry of Rain*

Tomorrow

tomorrow
i will take the
journey back
sail
the
middle passage

it
would be better
to be packed
like spoons again
than
to continue to
live among
knives and forks

Sand

under the suffocating
light of the sun
loneliness turns men
into sand

the desert
that separates
us
cannot be crossed

without
burning

Maintenance Man

with empty eyes
he lifts his
mop
out of
the bucket

water drips

cleaning
alone
in a tenement
hall

his
life
joins the
dust
in some
overlooked
corner

No Tacos for the Shah

i have not heard from miguel
in five weeks
i wonder where he is
miguel
so much like his uncle
so willing to help
i sneak across the border each week
to wash and iron clothes
i make a little money
not much
just a little money
enough to keep maria
from giving herself to the men
each night
i light a small candle for miguel
i watch it burn
like the inside of my womb
a soft wax dripping from between
my legs
the fire gone so long
the smoke of my husband
rising
across the border

The Weather

*For my people everywhere.*
—*Margaret Walker*

on elevators
on the bus
in front the store and house
old folks talk about the weather

rain and heat
all the time they talk
about the weather

once long ago
when no man owned the land
the color in the sky was filled with omens
a change in color
could feed or starve a man

when there was no rain
the ground cracked open
old folks took to sitting near the trees
there they would talk
about the weather

and when it rained
they would talk
about the land
the richness and the wealth
how the harvest
would be good

now on concrete streets
in rented homes
old folks curse the rain
they talk about the weather

they have no memory
of the land

Eric

dream
listen to nature's music
live among the earth creatures

fly over cities
let wings black the sun
we are africans
birds of flesh

travelers from another world
a place called dolphy

## Season of Hunger

the seasons turn
away from each other
the soul wanders at midnight
i watch the women of the village
empty the milk from their breasts
they have decided there will
be no children
they refuse to go to market
they sit near the river like rocks
some no longer speak to men
calling us famines
bad omens in this season of hunger

Silk

i have known women
to steal my heart and vanish
like master fard
in detroit around 1930

silks the only remains
of some lost religion
i've lost faith in

Solo
  *for Rhonda*

she has nothing to wear
only her dancing fits her body
the movement is all fabric
tight against the flesh
she moves from chair to bed
eyes like notes
soft
harmonic
playful

this is our solo
lips against lips
tongue against tongue

my fingers fingering her body

i play all melody
slow
fast
jazz and blues

i dress her with music.

press her breasts like keys

Slave Narratives
*for Gayle*

who is to say that your
letters to your lover
your poems
your sweet things
are not the makings of a slave narrative
a personal adventure
a journey to freedom
an account of how you outsmarted the master
how you cooked and cleaned until harriet called
you out the back door
who is to say that
you were not trapped in your own house
where every window faced south and you went to bed
dreaming of canada and divorce

Blues Go Find Another Color
                    *for S*

mercy

this woman who lives jazz
on the hudson
gives new jersey blues
and dirty weather

mercy

how she possesses me
with hidden cards and perfect hands
hoo-doo mama
if I ever met one

mercy

as I dance turn fall down
crawl just to knock on her
front door

mercy

when she flies away
leaving me with songs
too sad for words
blues walk outside
to find another color

mercy

Iran

a few days before the taking
of hostages in iran
i obtain a divorce from my wife
i leave the courthouse blindfolded
although i cannot see
i know that another fanatic is out there
ready to terrorize me with love
i quickly walk home
fearful of the next explosion

October 31
*for June*

tonight I have flashes
of being the streaks of silver
in your hair

Thulani

she was josephine baker
to those who knew who she was
her poems knew all the latest dances
when she read
white boys cried for tape recorders
her voice like a hot comb
moved through the blues
her hands improvised the latest jazz
she set the styles—the fashions
when she left we burned palm
scattered ashes
walked back into the wilderness

## Song for My Lady or Excuse Me McCoy

i am tired of women who love musicians
who desire to be loved by musicians
who think musicians are the best lovers
and the best players
i am tired
and do not care to listen to this anymore
do not sing to me or hum to me
or proclaim to me a new music
there is NO music
coltrane is dead
parker is dead
navarro is dead
young is dead
cannonball just died
and so have herbie sanders and benson
and I don't even listen to radio
i am so tired
of women sitting in clubs
sipping drinks of coke and rum
pretending to be billie bessie betty or whoever
laying around between acts
being very hip
i am very tired
of the woman who tells me that the man
she loves is in europe
back from europe
or heading for europe
i am tired of music lovers
coming down from new york
telling me about the apple
if you are william tell please do not take aim at my head
i am tired and need no second headaches
i do not need another woman to tell me
that what's hers belongs to the drummer
and what's mine is fine

but it just don't swing
i am tired of telling women
that I am better than bebop
that what I got is the new thing
that I can play an instrument as good as anyone
i am tired of telling them this
so from now on
whenever I hear a woman
talking about some musician
about how wayout his sound is
about how his music gets all up inside and moves her around
from now on when I hear a woman talking about a musician
i'm gonna turn my back like miles
pull my hat down like monk
disappear like rollins
and maybe come back next year
if I feel like it        and if she's ready

Panama

in the early twenties
a boat brought
my father to america
his first impressions
were spoken in spanish

years later when he
had forgotten the
language he could not
remember what he had

seen

Marathon

it's a strange time which finds me jogging
in early morning
the deadness of sleep alive in this world
the empty parks filled with unloved strangers
buildings gray with solitude
now near the end of another decade
i am witness to the loss of my twenties
a promise invisible
i run without purpose
far from the north star
i run with the sound of barking dogs closing in
i have lost count of the miles
i am older and nothing much matters
or has changed

Bronx Snapshot

andre's father
was from haiti

he was a happy man
who kept a jar
of white people
in his window

kept them in a
milk of magnesia
bottle

Bronx Sketches

I

in the bronx
between beck and kelly
streets
alberto once
believed to be
the cisco kid
filled his watergun
with pee
and shot our heads in

we smelled bad
for days but did
not die


II

once an old white
musician
who played the
accordion came to
the alley behind
our building

he played for coins

his head
became the target
for our garbage
when we found
we couldn't latin
to his sound

Cry of Rain

when I met him he was dead
his eyes like open graves
i threw flowers into them

    she was my only pallbearer
    lifting my coffin
    she placed it upon her head like fruit

    there were no crowds
    only soft moans from leaves
    catching wind

    soon I felt the darkness
    the covering
     the earth
     the faint cry of rain

Bojava

bojava put down his knife
splinters of wood
covered his boots
a few scraps caught in the fold of his pants
i took the walking stick from his hand
felt the smoothness rushing from the wood
take it bojava said
in time you will witness its power
you will come to understand
the wisdom I have carved

Midnight

I.

the wind naked
slammed its head
then its fist
into the side of the shack
shirley held the baby midnight to her breast
the rain fell hard outside
the nearby river was already swollen
water climbing over its banks
spilling across the land like pus from an
open wound
mr. jacobs had fought his way in from town
through the storm
to see how shirley and her new son were doing
that was four of maybe six hours ago
shirley now tried to keep midnight from crying
it was not easy
even for a woman her age
the weather was reason for concern
it was the worst storm she had ever witnessed
and the fear of a flood made it possible it would
be her last
shirley carried midnight to the window
she could barely
see the road outside
the rain was like a curtain one could not part
a casket one could not open
it prevented her from seeing the damage that had been done
in the distance shirley saw something coming towards her
shifting midnight to her right arm
she wiped the window with her left hand
it was hard to tell what it was
damn mr. jacobs out here again she thought
man done lost his mind

even a fool would have sense to keep his head dry
maybe he think I'm scared of the storm
the thought of mr. jacobs split in town
sliced by a cold knife of fear
shirley felt her head divide then open
she fell away from the window clutching
midnight

outside the shack
a winged horse spread its wings
the rider descending swiftly from its back
placed a flaming cross in front the door
shirley watched the flames dance
she felt the small body of midnight go limp in her hands
then saw her child turn to white dust
a powder falling to the floor

II

after shirley died
mr. jacobs was a different man
folks tried to comfort him after the funeral
but they would always leave when he started
cussing and swearing
once a strong man
mr. jacobs
now appeared to many to be a small boy
lost in the dark
trying to get home before midnight

III

no one could remember where the shack stood
they knew it was close to the river
no one knew or could remember
no one cared or went near

where the road turned
where it bent
like a tree stricken by the sickness of lightning

it was bojava
who one day gave us answers
who one day told us why
mr. jacobs wandered around town
sprinkling white powder on the ground
mumbling words and pointing his fist at the sky

Incantation
    *for Jonetta*

let all poems speak and address themselves
let each phrase like hair on a head
comb itself back madame walker style
let the love poems wear gardenias
let the political poems wear suits the way muslims did
during the days of elijah
let the poems be fruitful and multiple

## VI.
### *Where Are the Love Poems for Dictators?*

Juan

i meet juan
at the outskirts
of our village
we say nothing
walk to the water
where boats sleep
stuck in sand
we push one forward
into the smells of morning
check our nets
as the sun looks through
the openings in heaven

Senor Rodriguez

the old truck creaks
to the side of the road
victor the driver says we have to walk
the last miles to the fields
senor rodriguez refused to fix the truck again
he is an old man who sleeps with his money
now that his wife is dead
there are 12 men in victor's truck
another 30 somewhere in the dust ahead
we all carry machetes
the inside of our hands hard like the earth
we live on
our shirts hang from our chests like leaves too
tired to fall
i listen to victor curse the truck
the way I do the sun and senor rodriguez
in the middle of the afternoon
when sweat runs like rivers down the muscles
of my back and I have only prayers
to count the hours

Juanita

when she was small
she wore the lipstick of her mother
face made older with powder
like pictures of movie stars
cut from magazines
the blonde ones she taped on the  wall
next to jesus

## Madonna

four children on a blanket
eight children in a room
i sleep with my eyes open
the belly of jose swollen
like a half moon
there is no milk in my breasts
to comfort  his  needs
yesterday miguel walked to the city
to beg for food
it was his birthday
i had no gift
i prayed that miguel would not steal
the soldiers wait in doorways
they bring us bullets

Roberto

in chile
maria
holds
roberto
in her hands
in her hand
a photograph

gone
is the
laughter
& the smile
of our friend

when
i ask the authorities
about roberto
they shrug
their shoulders
they say
they have
not seen him

they ask
is he
missing

between
life & death
there are only
pictures

When Allende Was Alive

looking through the window of my country
i do not see myself outside
i trace the outline of my breath against glass
the cold enters my fingers

when allende was alive
i could open this window
look out across chile from my home in
santiago

there were no curtains to hide dreams
it was a time of hope

a time to press democracy against my lips
& hold her like a lover

Untitled

where are the love poems for dictators
i sit on a stool in a small room
no windows
i can touch walls without moving my arms
the smell of myself eats the last slice of air
in this prison
the food is terrible
it is a tasteless horror
in the next cell antonio weeps
his body already crushed by a thousand burns
at night i whisper poetry through the cracks
in the wall
my words like music kiss his eyes

Day of Protest / Night of Peace
*for Chile*

when the generals invite you home
do not salute them
when they ask you to forgive them
do not forgive them

there are too many missing graves
so few flowers left
there are families and bones broken
scattered across this land/world
where we live

when they invite you home
do not try and take all the things
you have found here

no

return home with all that you left
if only the promise to return
is all you took

Postcards from Miami

from the restaurant we could see
the hotel that survived the earthquake
further proof that this country
needed us    what could one buy now
except cheap jewelry and the latest
fashions from eastern europe    some
of us who stayed after the revolution
slept with postcard pictures of miami
over our heads    there are no clubs
and the movies come from cuba    still we meet
in the afternoon to drink and remember
the good days    the beer is warm and the wine
expensive    the good stuff was gone
long ago like lucille ball we try to
laugh and convince ourselves that life
too is filled with reruns

After the Generals

there are new slogans in the air & on the walls
i watch my mother working in the kitchen
she is slowly learning how to read
slowly stumbling out of the past
now & then she rests her head on the table
the pages of her notebook filled with promises
my mother can spell and read so few words
she tries to read the newspaper every day
& every day she has questions

how long will this revolution be?
when will we have more food?
why was manuel killed?
were not things better under the generals?

questions
& more questions
& questions I cannot answer

what do I tell my mother
a woman with so few tomorrows

how much forgiveness remains in her heart
& after the rule of generals
what is left to forgive

Nicaragua

what can i give you nicaragua
tears or blood
should i embrace you like i would
another man's wife
the shape of your back curving
against my hands
the brown earth color
of our meeting
on this loveless night

nicaragua
i have known prostitutes
I gave them money
now i look into the eyes of honduras
and costa rica
behind the headlines that hide behind
lies and something called america
a fruit filled with bones

nicaragua
if I never see the sun again
i will count your lovers among the
many that defended you
i will remember you dressing in the morning
near the window
i will remember your voice
and the way the wind carried your song
into the mountains

nicaragua
this poem is for our children
and your friend in managua who asked
me to live with her
whose face I wrapped in tissue
her hair like fine black thread

covering my shirts

this poem is for the poets
who will understand

Another Love Affair / Another Poem

it was afterwards
when we were in the shower
that she said

"you're gonna write a poem about this."

"about what?" i asked

## Art Is a Long Way from This Moment

if i didn't make up these poems
would you believe my life
the emptiness so rich it overflows
with loneliness     who are you
but a woman who walks inside her
own mystery     whose love is so
external it describes only gestures
you are the dream that did not last
the night     i am the man whose face
you will remember when your husband
returns from his affairs     let my
poems console you     here is the
pain i felt when you left

Playoffs

while i watch the playoffs
you use my phone to call
some other man

you stay until
the fifth inning
then you say you have
to leave

i watch you exit
like a pitcher heading
for the showers

somewhere someone
is keeping score

you perfect your game
with each man

love is the best curve
a woman can throw

Two Women: Or a Conversation with Sahara Nile

you need a change she said
why with horses dying in new york city and all
you need to leave this place

you need to find a small town out west
somewhere where a man can be a man
& women can be what they want to be

when i first needed it
lord—i can't even remember
but then when was the first time
you made love to a woman you really knew
& could remember her first name
as well as her middle initial &
other things most private

why i bet you never held a real woman
like me in your arms
look at you
you look like you looking for something
& not even god knows what it is
& you too dumb to ask for help
i tell you
you better stick your thumb out
& listen to miss sahara nile

why with horses dying from the heat & all
you don't need any more signs to tell you
love is difficult these days

now i love myself
& never loved my lovers
cause i love the truth more than i love a lie
now some men will warn you
before they harm you

the ones i know will simply ride you
until you die

we need a change she said
& she put her arms around me

Mississippi

death surrounds itself with the living
i watch them take the body from the house
i'm a young kid maybe five years old
the whole thing makes no sense to me
i hear my father say
    lord jesus – what she go and do this for
i watch him walk around the garden
kick the dirt
stare at the flowers
& shake his head   shake his head
he shake his head all night long

yazoo
jackson
vicksburg
we must have family in almost every city
i spent more time traveling than growing up
guess that's why i'm still shorter than my old man
he don't like to stay in one place much
he tell me

soon as people get to know your last name
seem like they want to call you by your first
boy   if someone ask you your name
tell them to call you mississippi
not sippi or sip but mississippi
how many colored folks you know name mississippi

none see

now you can find a whole lot of folks whose
name is canada
just like you can find 53 people in any phone book
whose name is booker t. washington

your mother she was a smart woman
gave you a good name
not one of them abolitionist names

what you look like with a name like
john brown or william lloyd garrison
that don't have no class

your mother she name you after the river
cause of its beauty and mystery
just like my mother named me nevada
cause she didn't know where it was

Only Language Can Hold Us Together

only language
can hold us together

i watch the women
bead their hair
each bead a word

braids becoming
sentences

she would
never comb her hair
it was always wild

like new poetry
it was difficult
to understand

she would enter
rooms where old women
would stare & mumble
& bold ones would say

"where's her mother"

she never understood why
no one ever understood the
beauty of her hair

like free verse
so natural as conversation
so flowing like the french
or spanish she heard or
overhead she thought she knew

"i want to go to
mozambique" she said one day

combing her hair
finding the proper beads
after so long

"i want to go to
mozambique " she said

twisting her hair
into shape the way her
grandmother made quilts
each part separated &
plaited

"i want to go to
mozambique or zimbabwe
or someplace like luanda

i need to do something
about my hair

if only i could
remember

the words
to the language
that keeps
breaking in my
hands"

Tao

the
woman
who calls
herself
a buddhist
follows
me
home

## Poem Written on the 4th of July

& if i did leave
where would my leaving take me
into last week's argument or
maybe the first night we made
love

this is for the moment:
the making of a wrong turn
the asking for directions

Elaine Beckford

when the dog needed walking
we would walk the dog
out near the river where the johnsons lived
and the rich folks had summer homes
and maybe a few of us like ginger and eddie
would toss rocks into the water
take our shoes off
splash each other and try to scoop
small fish up with our hands
our world was perfect
like sunlight coming through the curtains
and finding a special spot on the wall or floor
i never had goosebumps until the summer the
body of elaine beckford was found in the water
near the big rock and police came and told my daddy
to keep us indoors and it was three weeks later
that they shot a colored man
a few miles from where we lived
some of our neighbors said he was innocent
but most folks said he was only colored
and someone had to pay for doing what they did
to elaine beckford     let it be the colored
my daddy said and no one knew but me
that my daddy was real sweet on elaine
and i caught them twice together in the barn
she no older than i
and I don't know what they doing
cause i ain't old enough to know

Tyrone

nothin like the smell that comes from fresh cut wood
i like workin with my hands
building and takin things apart
when my daddy was alive i was always in the toolbox
askin questions and tryin to build what i could
when I got my own place i was almost thirty
went out to john barker's store one day to get supplies
that's where I met my wife margaret
she's a nice shape thing that stays in coveralls
hair cut so short you think she's a boy
john ask about her and i tell him she's tryin to get the garden goin
i get back to my place about three in the afternoon
john gave me a good deal
said it was the best wood i could get without going down to the valley
well i start to unload this timber
and where john had it tied it came loose and so the whole thing
give way and knock me down
i could hear the bone break in my leg when the first piece
of wood land on it
margaret come runnin from around the back of the house
her scream is like someone's gun being fired in the woods
i try to get her to calm down and finally she does
but i know she ain't
my daddy once told me some trees
got the devil in them
and when you go to hammer a nail
the nail breaks
and you stand there cussin the wood unaware that something
is  listenin to you
you  can tell bad wood just by rubbin your hand on it
or when you cut it and it don't smell good
i took some of john's lumber and built a fence around
margaret's garden
that was two months ago
you can go out there yourself and you won't see nothin growin

i tell margaret it's the wood makin everything die
she said that's nonsense
well i wish my daddy was alive to tell her otherwise

# A Walk in the Daytime Is Just as Dangerous as a Walk in the Night

a simple dirt road
surrounded by all these mountains
trees and lakes
does not offer calmness
to my soul or mind
even here in upstate new york
the stillness drives a fear
through my heart like mississippi
or history and i cannot walk
without hearing the barking of dogs
or the yell from some redneck
screaming "there he goes"
i try to accept all these things
as irrational fears that
i should enjoy this time in the
country to relax and be at peace
with myself and i am happy
to be out walking in the morning
on this road which runs into
route 28 near eagle lake
not far from the small town
where i plan to purchase stamps
and postcards and while
i'm walking along the highway
feeling good about the weather
and thinking about nothing in particular
two vans filled with people
speed by and disturb the quiet and call me
   "nigger"
and the peaceful walk is no more
and in the midst of all this
beautiful scenery i become a woman
on a dark city street vulnerable
to any man's attack
it is not yet mid-afternoon

but the virginity of my blackness
has been raped
and this is no longer
a simple walk into town
this is like every walk i have taken
in my life wherever and whenever
i have been alone and my fears are
as real as this dirt beneath
my feet

*VII.*
*First Light*

The Things in Black Men's Closets

on the top shelf
of the closet
is the hat my father
wears on special occasions
it rests next to the large jar
he saves pennies in

his head is always bare
when i see him walking
in the street

i once sat in his bedroom
watching him search
between sweaters and suits
looking for something missing
a tie perhaps

then he stopped
and slowly walked to the closet
took the hat from the shelf

i sat on the bed
studying his back
waiting for him to turn
and tell me who died

Night

at some ungodly hour
her house shoes would scrape across
the wooden floor
as she moved from bedroom to kitchen
i would lie in my room and hear her
opening cabinets
washing dishes
placing a pot on the stove
then walking slowly back to where i was
to see how i was sleeping
to see if any blankets were on the floor

Fire

i am ten years old
and share a room with my brother.
at seventeen he dreams of becoming
a priest or monk.  i am too young
to know the difference. in our room
the small bureau is an altar covered
with white cloth. two large candles
stand on each end. my fear of fire
begins in this room.

Growing Up

the day my mother
threw away my comic books
and encouraged me to read the bible
was the day i gave up being
a superhero and started to think
of miracles

this is how i came to love you
like moses looking over his
shoulder before he left that
mountain

Faith: My Brother Richard Returns Home from the Monastery

i was not home
my mother, sister and i
had gone to the store
only my father was home

how happy he must have been
to open the door and see
his first born

to give your son
up to the lord is one thing
to receive him back is another

i would not have been surprised
if my father had lived the
rest of his life on his knees
i knew how grateful he was

faith is the meaning of love
between men

Men

my father and brother
have no wings
their legs are short
and cannot reach the ground

when i left home
i left walking on my head
i decided i would give birth
to a leopard

i stopped at the place
where the river disappears
into the sky

those of us who are birds
envy the leopard
even the strange ones
who call themselves men
hide inside their shells

First Light

*for Denise*

the cat opens the door to the bedroom
i see you sleeping alone
the covers hiding your face
it is a few hours before first light
today is mother's day
there is unfinished work on my desk
a few unpaid bills
i have been reading raymond carver
how does a man give birth to a poem?
with difficulty and great anticipation

Jasmine

on my desk is a small bottle
which once held perfume
inside is the cord that joined
my wife and daughter

it is strange that i keep it

my mother kept my brother's
sixth finger in a jar stuffed
with cotton

one night i found it
while secretly searching
for cookies hidden in a drawer
filled with underwear
why do we keep things that are not ours?

in another land
an old woman would take this cord
and place it in the earth

tomorrow when my daughter becomes a woman
i will give her this small bottle
filled with the beginnings of herself

on that day she will hold love
in her hands

The Second Child
*for Nyere-Gibran*

in sports they say it's difficult
to repeat, to win, to gain a championship
two consecutive years; so it is with children,
the difference, the new season, the second child.

each beginning finds a newborn, a rookie
struggling to learn the lessons of spring,
a time of hope and expectations, of fingers
gripping and pulling things to mouth.

## Bill Mazeroski Returns Home from the World Series

when i was a kid
i told my old man
that i would make a name for myself
like walter next door who had a hit
record on the radio for two weeks
and then enlisted and got himself shot

i want people to forget eisenhower
i want them to remember my swing
the way i touched third and headed
home to every fan in the world

Grow Your Own Chinese Vegetables

i suffer slowly now
pain without swelling
evenings without horizons
the dog sits by the door
too tired to walk itself
plants hang from windows
your photograph walks
across the room
and picks out another record
in the kitchen i teach myself
to grow chinese vegetables
across the street
the bus stop practices
meditation
rosa parks laughs at willie mays
losing his cap
it's terrible how these things
happen

Malcolm X, August 1952

i suppose i should be
grateful to the white man
letting me out. where can
a black man in america go?
i stand with the prison in
my shadow. elijah muhammad
teaches us that we are not
thieves. we are the lost ones
who have been stolen.

allah bless my tongue as it
prepares to heal. there are
so many who are in need of
the message. i feel this
country changing.  the cross
no longer ours to bear.

## Atlantic City

we drove north to new jersey
we had our friend carla's car. aisha's
brother had been killed in newark. shot
five times in the head.  she talked
about her family while i drove. i don't
like any of them, she said.  i don't know
why i'm going to the funeral.  maybe we
should go to atlantic city, she joked.
i thought it was a good idea. she never
told me her brother's name. it didn't
matter. life is luck, a name nothing but
chance.

Rafael

the day
rafael was pushed
from the roof we knew
he was different. we knew
he could die and we could
live. live to laugh at him
begging for his life. how
stupid he looked, handsome
face and all. what a pity
to be so beautiful and not
be able to fly.

## The Door

the day after the national election
the sky cleared and the sun found its guitar.
i ran to the plaza and soon discovered myself
dancing in the middle of a jublilant crowd.
a nation of song, a nation of thousands pushing
like the sea to the cathedral. i felt the sweet
sweat of arms, legs and chests. i found my place
among the living, the dead, the ghosts, the children
waiting to be born. something more powerful than
victory was in the air. i could breathe again.
my prison door was open. my country was outside.
she had been waiting for me.

## The Sea

neruda once told me
that i should visit the sea
that to know a wave is to love
is to come and flow from one to another
the sand is like our hearts
so many parts to care for
so endless and yet it touches the sea
as one

Personal #1975

when
between
her
legs
i think
of scissors
cutting

The Feeling of Jazz

what would ellington
say if he saw us walking
across his bridge?  your
hands pushed deep into
your pockets. my hat a
funny one like the kind
musicians wear. i can
see duke being majestic,
wondering if we're lovers.
how else to explain this
closeness between our coats.

Survival Poem
*for June*

when the earth opened
i whispered your name
i prayed for your safety
the distance between us
a slight tremor
our love holding up
against the odds

## Chinatown

in the morning
she would hold his
hands against the light
translucent hands like the torn
shade at her window
in the morning
she would hold his hands
against the light
like fans from the orient
she would hold them close
to her face

Rebecca

will i hate mirrors?
will i hate reflections?
will i hate to dress?
will i hate to undress?

jim my husband
tells me it won't matter
if i have one or two
two or one it doesn't matter
he says

but it does
i know it does

this is my body
this is not south africa or nicaragua
this is my body
losing a war against cancer
and there are no demonstrators outside
the hospital to scream stop

there is only jim
sitting in the lobby
wondering what to say
the next time we love
and his hands move towards
my one surviving breast

how do we convince ourselves
it doesn't matter?
how do i embrace my own nakedness
now that it is no longer complete?

*VIII.*
*Whispers, Secrets and Promises*

Whispers, Secrets and Promises

afternoon
and your eyes walk
across the table into
my hands

this is the beginning
of confessions and faith
or how you braid your
hair

a metaphor
for things left
unsaid

Ask Me Now

like Thelonius Monk

I record my love for you
and no one understands it

the complexity of my
declarations

the strange way
it makes you feel

Meal

1 Man
1 Woman
2 Bowls of Soup
1 Piece of Bread

Love fills
2 spoons

Conversation

I told her... she had very nice hips.
She told me...I shouldn't be looking around
corners.

I said...I like to see where I'm going.

I Have Always Wanted a Woman to Be My Lover

How can it be morning in two places at once?
I was so happy when I moved into this house.
Finally a place where I can grow and hang my plants.
Finally a lover to love my difference and my sex;
her tongue discovering the secret parts of me.
I have always wanted a woman to be my lover.
How many men find this strange?
Once, my father found his way to my bed.
He was not lost. I did not surrender.
I fought and was beaten and wet my bed with his blood.

Now a woman holds a knife to my throat
and I am speechless...

I did not know she would do such things.
How unnatural for a woman to beat another woman
after being lovers. Did she not whisper one night
when I was in her arms—no man would ever treat me
better?

How We Sleep on the Nights We Don't Make Love

One night
I looked into my parent's bedroom.
It was a night when I was home from college.
They were sleeping on opposite sides of the bed.
My father's arm almost touching the floor.
My mother snoring and shaking, one hand under her breast.
The room was dark but I could see how much older they had
become during my few months away.
They slept like strangers in a bus terminal or on a plane.
I refused to believe they were lovers.
I closed the door in order to keep their secrets.

Terrorism

my mother did not need terrorism
to feel unsafe in New York.
when I was a boy someone was always
getting stuck in the elevator. we
lived in the projects in the South
Bronx. this was before Soweto and
after Sharpsville. my mother first
believed the neighborhood was changing
when she could no longer obtain fresh
meat from the corner store.

Aaron

after watching
heston part the
red sea for the
first time
my brother ran
to his room
and pulled the
blanket from
his bed

he stood in the
doorway proudly
proclaiming
himself moses

he was the
oldest so what
he said was law
for my sister
and me

later that night
while my brother
slept I crawled
into his bed and
picked the lint
from his hair

Departures & Arrivals

My mother and I are at the train
station. She is returning to New
York. We are early so I leave her
sitting on a bench alone. I walk
over to where the telephones are
and strike a pose of a movie
star waiting to kiss a lover good-bye.
I don't smoke so I have no cigarette
to dangle from my hands or lips.
I stare at my mother sitting on the
bench. She is talking to herself.
I think how crazy she looks. She
clutches her pocketbook fearful
of strangers. She looks at me with
eyes that forget I am her son.
It has always been this way.
One of us going somewhere without
the other.

My Father Is Washing His Face

My father is washing his face
I listen to the water splashing in the sink
He rubs his hands together with soap
It is always Ivory Soap that makes his beard white
My father looks young for his age
This is something people always mention
When they see him
Especially relatives who gather at funerals
And weddings
My father's face is a reminder
Of what it means to be young
I am happy when someone says
I look like my father or when my
Father reminds me to wash my face
And I reach for the soap in his hand

When We Are Alone

I let the children
climb into my bed. They
are afraid to sleep alone.
It is dark and they cannot
see. I feel their small bodies
against mine. A foot pushes into
the center of my chest. I tickle
it and it moves away to join a
silly laugh.

Tonight is a night for stories
and tales filled with monsters
and those funny space things. I tell
my children to hush and listen.

The stories begin
when we are alone and afraid
of the dark. We need the stories
to hold us. We need the words to
keep us warm.

Science

When you were in elementary school
no one told you about the black laws
of cause and effect. Your science teacher
failed to teach you about why a police
club struck against a black man's head
in the south resulted in a house burning
down in the north or how prejudice could
make a store clerk's smile turn into a
coldness below freezing. You often
wondered while waiting in line how you
could become invisible to every atom in
the world. You tried to understand the
reason for your condition. All the blues
you knew couldn't defy gravity. All the
jazz you heard couldn't keep you from
exploding like a star.

Sidewinder, 1972

Lee Morgan dead and my roommate
decides he can't wait for graduation.
Packing his horn and clothes, he tells
me to keep the books. School is out.
Music has a gun to his head. I try to
tell him jazz is just another woman
with beautiful legs.

Angela

I was too young to do the Lord's work
so they left me by the side of the road
and went walking off into the sunset
the shade of the car and the heat from
my own breath stuck on my tongue
like the words from the good book

They had a callin'
first my momma and then my daddy
someone called out their names
telling them there were things to be done
and this was the time for miracles to be believed

My daddy took the rifle from the basement
and I watched him bless it at the dinner table
telling my momma that this here should be the
tool they should give thanks for

I was five years old and could not reach
the butter or the bread and my momma asked
my daddy if this was the right thing to do

I still remember the silent look
he gave her and Jeff down the road gets
that look every time he sees a stray dog
so I know it's best for my momma to say amen
if she don't want an argument and to simply
trust in the Lord and in my daddy's house
the Lord wears blue underwear and watches tv

And I ask my momma to pass the bread
and daddy he put the gun down in the chair
next to me like it was my brother or sister and
it sat next to me while I ate and all the time
I kept asking myself why and when

We gonna go on a trip to the mountains
and give ourselves to the Lord my daddy finally say
he belch it out like he finished his food
but his plate still has meat and gravy on it

We gonna go to the mountains
and give ourselves to the Lord this evening
the world don't need us here no more
he ask my momma to fetch the bibles
and I say I'll help since we have bibles everywhere
where other folks have clothes and furniture we have bibles
hundreds of them

And my momma always tells me to trust in the good book
and I wonder which one
but this evening it don't matter cause
I'm  scared and don't know what I believe
and when my daddy says he's ready to kill himself
let's go

I fall down on my knees and start crying
I can't pray to the Lord cause the Lord
done blessed my daddy and besides
I'm just a child and who would listen to me
and that's when my daddy says to my momma –
maybe she ain't ready to do the Lord's work
what you think?

And my momma looked at me like she was standing
over me in the bathtub studying me close
looking for some spot of dirt that I missed
and she pause and says softly
maybe she ain't ready
no—I don't think she's ready yet

Which is why they left me here by the side of the road
by the car with a box of bibles

and I watched my daddy lead my momma
towards the mountain
one hand on her shoulder and the other on his gun
and I don't know how far they got before they disappeared
cause I was crying like a lost sheep or maybe a stray dog
one that Jeff could find
I prayed for Jeff to find me cause I believed
the Lord already knew where I was

Houston
Christmas Eve 1954

Big Mama Thornton
sitting backstage
with Johnny Ace
nothing to do
but sing the blues
and put a gun to
your head

Roy Campanella: January, 1958

Night as dark as the inside
of a catcher's mitt.
There are blows I can take
head on and never step back
from. When Jackie made the news
I knew I would have a chance
to play in the majors.
Ten years ago I put the number
39 on my back and tonight God
tries to steal home.

I've Been Waiting for a Letter from You

The wind blows a newspaper down the street
Four boys bounce a ball on the gray sidewalk
It's Friday afternoon and school is out
The mailman stops and opens the mailbox
I've been waiting for a letter from you
Here comes Maggie Anderson from the store
Her husband is still looking for a job
Late tonight they will drink and love and fight
It was that way before you went away
The sky is dark and rain is coming down
I close my window and pull down the shade
The bed in my room cries itself to sleep

A Painting of a Street in Black and Blue

I can feel the summer nights growing cold
The brown leaves falling to the ground from trees
A man walks his dog to the corner store
I watch it bark and jump and fight its leash
Across the street a small boy begs for change
His mother bends and wipes his mouth with love
On the stoop two old men share wine and smoke
Police drive by in their black and white cars
In the above apartment a blues crime
A young man moaning for a woman gone

## A House in Provincetown

where the two streets meet
there is a house where our hands first met
and behind the house there is the water as
beautiful as when i first looked into your eyes
and wanted to swim naked into the rest of you

i remember the snow falling outside
as early as the first days of february
and we found warmth on the floor and i
rested on my back and felt the soft feet of
your hair walk across my chest

## In Small Town USA

in small town usa
it doesn't matter if you can count
all the black people on one hand
and have a finger for yourself
it's 7 am and you look out the window
of your hotel and there's an old black
woman coming to work to scrub and clean
and this woman reminds you of your mother
tired but getting to work early and on time
never late as you close the curtain
and climb back into bed knowing you are
not alone and this woman is nearby
getting things ready for you and when you
leave your room you make your bed
and fold your towels hoping in this
small way to make it easier for this
woman you now pass in the hall
and you both wonder who will speak first
during this moment when being black is
all there is

The Women
*Ah Beautiful you are, my love, beautiful you are.*
    *— The Song of Solomon* 1:15

I.
My braids are extensions of my mother's hands.
The roots of my hair are my beginnings.

II.
My sister is my best friend, my best friend is my sister.
We hold hands, we embrace, we kiss.
We are sisters and so is our love.

III.
When I see myself I dance.

IV.
I will never lose my beauty.
The wrinkles in my skin are the rivers of life.

Urban Zen

I.
my blood
in the street
on our block

II.
beer
bottles
covering
the
cement
grass

III.
car
alarm
ringing
who
hears?

IV.
two
quarters
in my pocket
spare change
for he who
asks

V.
on the bus
no room
still we
stop
for
more

VI.
card
board
instead
of glass
for a window

VII.
my
neighbor
moved
to
where?

## Black Boys

young black boys
sitting with their
backs against a wall
sneakers sparkling
while others stand
with hands pushed
deep into jeans
pants resting on
their hips as casual
as gunfire

Sponge

on the corner we called him sponge
because he didn't bleed like many
of us who were shot several times
and died too young to brag to show
the healed flesh wounds on basketball
courts in summertime or to girls
whose bodies covered ours on hot nights
and voices slipped and fell with each
breeze from one house to another

sponge shot twice in the alley with ellis
fell down and saw his hands absorb
the blood of his brother like a straw
this was something  that made us believe
in jesus and others mentioned how farrakhan
was last seen being lifted up by a spaceship

in our school books we searched for the
first pages of this new testament

Freedom

after word spread
about emancipation
some of us went to
the end of the
plantation and looked
for our children to
return. freedom don't
mean much if you can't
put your arms around it.

Mountain Wife

in the yard
the truck sits stuck in mud
the hood bleeding from the last accident
I tell Carrie not to play near her daddy
not when he drunk or can't find work
I yell at her but she can't hear
ears deaf from my own screams
I wash our clothes with my tears
the hardness of my hand like his
I pass the mirror in the bedroom
and I recognize my mother's face
my husband sleeping in his clothes
just like my daddy did and now I dry
between my legs while praying
his spit won't make me pregnant

For June

If I had met you
in '60 or '61
I would have given
you Valentine cards
made out of construction
paper and cut into
apple-shaped hearts

I would have handed
over my Willie Mays
and Warren Spahn
baseball cards
my best cat-eye marble
even two Almond Joys
a Milky Way
and some Twinkies

Baby—I would have
loved you

given you everything

all this
and more

Chalk

the women on the bus wore no stockings.
it was winter and their legs were covered
with a white layer of ash, almost like snow.
things were changing and I took this to be
another sign of change, a reason for so much
death during this time of trouble and despair.
for days the news remained the same and I took
to reading my bible. I felt older now and more
vulnerable. when I went to work or to the store
my back was bent, my head low, my eyes afraid
of strangers, even friends. I was alone and my
community had become a place of darkness, of shadows
of hopelessness and unexplainable occurrences. I took
to keeping a journal, a written record of the drought.
there were streets in the city where there were no
trees or grass or growing things. only a white dust
like chalk, a film, a layer of death covering the
blackness of my flesh and memories of who
we were and what we had become.

Salat

poetry is prayer
light dancing inside words

five times a day
I try to write

step by step
I move towards the mihrab

I prepare to recite
what is in my heart

I recite your name

*IX.*
*Buddha Weeping in Winter*

Morning Buddhism

in the yard
dead leaves
from last night's winds

I sweep small twigs
and branches into a pile

in the house
everyone is sleeping

on a table a cup filled
with tea and honey

the newspaper sections
scattered across the
floor

Altar

shaman
builds
altar

pictures
poems
cards
letters

waiting
for the
sacred
fire

Stem in Search of Bowl

I am
stem

hollow

blow
love

hear
music

dance

Flower Wife

walk
sacred

find a flower
wife

marry
her
fragrance

Devotion

I share
this
earth
walk

with you

I bow
my head
and drink
from your
bowl

Buddha Without a Head

in sierra leone
a soldier cuts off
the arms of a child

the soldier is a
buddha without
a head

Dear Flower Wife

if the winds of my heart cause pain
it is because of this earth walk
do not lose your petals of love
sun and rain will dance one day

Buddha Weeping in Winter

snow falling on prayers
covering the path
made by your
footprints

i wait for spring
and the return of love

how endless
is this whiteness
like letters without
envelopes

# X.
*How We Sleep on the Nights We Don't Make Love*

Hi J
I Decided to Rewrite What I Sent to You
*for June Jordan*

our friendship
is what keeps us whole
love is essential as air

prayer contains desire
to worship is to open
the door to one's heart

we were looking at
the ceiling and then
we saw the sky

May 26, 2002

The Lakers won tonight because
Robert Horry hit a three pointer
at the buzzer. I miss you.
I'm always touching your rim
and slipping out. Maybe it's my
east coast style or John Coltrane
playing "Too Young To Go Steady"
on his Ballads album. Sometimes
the music bounces like a ball and
love is something you can't catch
so you keep shooting.

## A Portrait in Nine Lines

I want to hold your face in my hands
just for its laughter. I love your hat.
I was standing in a bookstore when
you turned the corner. Page after page
reminds me of your arms. The wind
sits in a park reading a book of your
poems. Is today your birthday? Yes
is such an easy word to say. I know
this is the portrait of you I love.

A Portrait of Yes in Fourteen Lines

I want to hold your face in my hands
and share my laughter with your eyes.
I love your hat. I can see your hair
giving my heart directions again. I was
standing in a bookstore across town
when I turned and found
my way to the poetry section. I like
how poem after poem reminds me of
your arms. I once sat in a park
reading about birds. I was hungry for
love. I cried when the crumbs were
gone. I thought today was your birthday.
I had a present for you. I know this poem
will say yes to everything you do.

Kiss

three times I wanted
to kiss you

place my hand
on your breast

the tip of your nipple
finding my palm

and wearing it
like a hat

what should my
other hand wear?

my fingers so wet
from your rain

What Does the E Stand For?

Everything
Each eye exists embracing exceptional emerald evenings
Evolution explains Eden's evil
Earth's ecology equates exploitation evaporation
Errors ending evergreen elms
Escort elephants eagles elks eastward
Enlightenment echoes Ezra Ezekiel
Enlist Esther Eugene Ethan Edward Ellington
Enough English explanations ecco
Exit eternity
Elucidate Ethelbert elucidate
E evokes every ecstatic emotion

Toothpaste

after dinner
you have the habit
of curling up in
the couch
like a tube of
toothpaste all bent
funny and nice
I like to brush
after every meal

Honey

Your petals open
Sweet honey inside of you
My tongue licks the jar

The Seduction of Light

I place your slippers together and place them
in the corner. I make the bed. I touch the place
where you slept. There is only a trace of you.
A wet towel, a tube of toothpaste, a comb with
your hair – still wet. I stop and think of how little
we talk. I hear the dripping from the bathroom
faucet, the dog barking next door. Through the
curtains sunlight stretches and spreads herself
across the rug. So seductive is light whenever
she places a hand on a wall. I wait inside the
room curling against a picture like smoke. The
end of love is a photograph found in a wallet.
I reach into my pockets for my keys. I am leaving.
I slip my shoes on.

Drummers?

the heart
is a drum

but
who will teach us
to listen?

what sound
will it make?

love?

how deaf
we are

Rosa Parks Dreams

Rosa Parks dreams about
a bus in Jerusalem. A headless
woman sits in her seat. There is no
driver today. The top of the bus
is missing. On the road a line
of bodies segregated from the living.
They sleep against a twisted metal
frame. Wild flowers stare from
a field.

Honey & Watermelons

A man is making a bomb.
His slender fingers
are like threads and wires
weaving into metal.

The man is not thinking
of destruction or how a
child might lose a limb
or a mother a child.

He is thinking of honey
and watermelons and a
countless number of virgins
to hold his hands.

The man is thinking of
paradise and how this life
is an illusion and what
he is making is not a bomb.

On the table next to his
tools is a book filled
with wonder and miracles
he cannot understand.

The man is hungry for
the next life so he
completes his work
and cleans his table.

A man is walking down
the street with a bomb.
He stops next to a man
who looks like me.

## Malik

Malik mumbled Arabic
over his plate like someone
adding salt before tasting.
Islam had been good to him.
It was light slipping
between prison bars,
changing shadows into prayer
rugs.

When Malik thought about the
murder he had committed
his hands tightened around his
Quran and Mecca seemed as
far away as freedom.

A few guards and prisoners
thought Malik's new faith
was a gimmick, a safety device
or a wall to protect one's back
from a punch.

Renee who called herself Malik's
girlfriend still wore short skirts
when she went to see him.
It was her way of slapping the face
of God for taking her man away.

Freedom Candy

*So what kind of name is Omar?*
I ask this new boy at school.
*You named after a candy bar or what?*
*You know you too light to be milk chocolate.*

Omar looks at me and laughs.
Since that first smile he's my best friend
maybe my best friend ever.

Folks call us the inseparables
like one of those old singing groups
my daddy is always talking about.

Omar is a Muslim name Omar tells me.
I think it still sounds like a candy bar,
like O'Henry, Baby Ruth, Mars or Almond Joy.

Maybe his momma should have named him
Snickers because of the way he laughs.
Omar's name sounds like candy
and the way he acts is sweet to me.

Every teacher except Mrs. Greenfield thinks so.
Mrs. Greenfield she don't like Muslims
and the rest of us she calls natural born sinners
because of the way we talk and behave.

Omar says we should tell Mrs. Greenfield
about herself since it's Black History Month.
So Omar stands up and says to Mrs. Greenfield

*How come you don't lead us somewhere?*
*Why you not like Harriet Tubman?*
*Why no field trips?*
*Why no trips to the museum or zoo?*

*Why we never go nowhere, why?*

Mrs. Greenfield, she don't say nothing.
She just looks at Omar as if he is the last Muslim
on earth and is about to die.

I think of how Omar says Muslims pray
five times a day and how cats have nine lives and
just maybe Omar might make it to 3 o'clock
or maybe he won't.

Suddenly Mrs. Greenfield has one of those
fainting spells just like old Moses Tubman.
She has to sit down behind her desk so
she tells me to go get her some water.

I feel free as I race down the hall
wondering how Omar can be sweet sometimes
and get on everyone's nerves the next.

My daddy once told me M&Ms
melt in your mouth and your hands
especially if you colored.

Wait until I tell Omar.

Sister Sheba, Omar & Me

Sister Sheba
She's my cousin
She lives across town
where my momma tells me not to go
not unless it's daytime
and the sun is out bright

*Don't you go over there*
*without asking,* my momma say
And when I ask her she tells me *no*
so I don't ask no more
You know what I mean?

And so I have to wait for Sister Sheba
to come see me and tell me everything
my momma don't want me to know

*So why you have a Muslim for a friend?*
she asks me the next weekend my aunt visits
my momma and Sister Sheba visits me

Sister Sheba
she's always trying to get into your business
which is why she don't have no time for herself
Her hair be flying all different ways and my
momma don't even want to let her in the house
and if she see her outside she don't say she's
family because why embarrass yourself in public
if you don't have to
That's what my momma say
and that's what Anna Banana says too

Anna Banana is my guidance counselor
Her real name is Mrs. Bernstein
but everyone calls her Anna Banana

because she's always telling kids

that if they would give up
junk food and just eat fruits
and vegetables everything would be
OK in school

Our grades would improve and we would have
what she calls self esteem and be like white
kids which is crazy to me since we're all black
and that's why we call Mrs. Bernstein Anna
Banana and my momma calls her a real fruitcake
and says *that woman shouldn't even be around*
*kids let alone trying to guide them somewhere*
And today Sister Sheba
sounds just like Anna Banana
asking why I have a Muslim for a friend

She saw Omar in my house last month
and asked me where his shoes were and I said
*They by the front door, didn't you see them*
*when you came in?*

Omar takes off his shoes
whenever he comes to see me
just like in the mosque he's always talking
about and I ain't seen because my momma
say *boy you was a problem in my womb and*
*so I don't need you around no strange influences*
So I don't get to go to the mosque with Omar
but he gets to play with me because momma say
*That boy should have some fun*
*most Muslims I see don't even smile* she tells me

*What the Lord give you teeth for*
*if you can't smile?*

So I tell Sister Sheba
to get her face out of mine and leave Omar alone
and why she can't mind her own business when
she visits is beyond me

Omar says I should pray or do salat
something like that because Sister Sheba
lives where the bad boys are

Omar says she's gonna have a baby and maybe
never finish school
I tell Omar to *Shhhhhhhhhh…and hush his face*
Sometimes Omar can be a real Anna Banana
but he still my best friend
my best friend ever or what my momma calls
an apple in the hands of Eve

Hmmm
I wonder what my momma means by that
You think Mrs. Bernstein knows?

Omar, Books & Me

Folks call Omar a bookhead and me a bookend.
I don't read too much because I don't have time.
I don't even wear a watch to remind myself.

Why should I look at lines
on a page if they don't move
like the movies?

Omar reads so much about black history
and black heroes, I tell him he's gonna
be left behind living in a pyramid or something.

Omar says he looks Egyptian and maybe I should
look in the mirror and find myself too.
He laughs at me and takes a swing at my head.

*You gonna be a bookend forever with folks*
*pushing you out the way like you at the end*
*of the shelf of life.*

I listen to Omar and shake my head.
The end of the shelf of life sounds
like one of those soap shows Natalie watches.

She's always crying about some fool in love.
Omar says Natalie is my other bookend
and maybe that's why I'm afraid of books.

I laugh and tell him Natalie is his girlfriend.
*You read your face Omar.*
*Boy, you should read your face.*

I run down the street with my sneakers untied,
tripping over myself and being silly.
Omar runs after me shouting about how he plans

to bookmark my butt.
*You too slow and can't run,* I holler.
*I'm running to the end of the world.*

I turn the corner
as fast as Omar
can turn a page.

The Equator

*So what's that line around your nose*
*the equator or something?*  I'm in the playground
sitting next to Omar and in between him and Natalie.

She's the new girl
with the old clothes who moved into
the corner house one month ago.

*What you talking about?* she squeaks.
Her voice has that little girl sound
like she could sing high notes

and maybe call herself Mariah
but she's just Natalie
from down the street.

*Why you staring at my nose?  You just*
*a silly looking boy with one of those*
*Mooslem hats on your head.*

*You shouldn't even be looking at me.*
*Why should I let you look at me?*
*Why? You tell me why?*

I'm between Omar and Natalie and this
is what my Momma means when she says
*If you make your bed you gotta lie in it.*

Or maybe this is just a hard place
and the rock is here too.
I don't know.

It was me who decided not to do my homework,
so here I am listening to Omar trying to talk
all smart and talk about geography

like he knows where he is.
Omar don't know nothing about no equator.
*You can't see the equator fool!* I tell him.

*You just want to mess with Natalie's nose.*
In between my words, her tears gather like
clouds coming from behind the big buildings

and telling us it's time to go.
But it's Natalie's crying which makes me shiver.
She stutters and tries to find her own rain of words.

*My daddy broke my nose when I was small*
*because I didn't stop crying.*
*He broke my nose and it left a mark.*

Natalie's words catch Omar and me like we
were running and now we both out of breath.
Omar pushes me out the way and puts his arm

around Natalie's shoulder like he's the equator.
I guess this was the right thing to do
if we added our ages together.

Sometimes Omar does things I wish I could do.
Sometimes he just sees things
I'm too young to see.

Looking for Omar

I'm in the school bathroom
washing my hands without
soap but I'm still washing my hands.

I turn the water off
and look for a paper towel
but paper towels have been gone
since the first day of school
and it's June now.

I start to leave the bathroom
with my wet hands but then
the big boys come in talking
loud and cussing like they
rap stars or have new sneakers.

I hear the one named Pinto
talking about how someone
should get Omar after school
since he's the only Muslim they know.

Pinto talks with an accent
like he's new in the neighborhood too.

I don't have to ask him
what he's talking about
since everybody is talking
about the Towers and how they
ain't there no more.

My momma said it's like
a woman losing both
breasts to cancer and my daddy
was talking at the dinner table
about how senseless violence is

and Mrs. Gardner next door lost
two tall boys to drive-bys.

Bullets flying into
both boys heads
making them crumble too.

Everybody around here is
filled with fear and craziness
and now Pinto and the big boys
thinking about doing something bad.

I stare at my wet hands
dripping water on my shoes
and wonder if I should run
and tell Omar or just run.

I feel like I'm trapped
in the middle of one of those
bible stories but it ain't
Sunday.

I hear my momma's voice
saying

*Boy, always remember to wash*
*your hands but always remember*
*you can't wash your hands from*
*everything.*

Rebecca Lets Down Her Hair

I am a victim
of my own war
as I stand in the
shower watching
my hair fall and
swim

Is this worse
than cancer
this loss of
hair?

Why do I
think of balding
men in war
camps and
Japanese
women after
the bomb?

I love
my hair
as much
as life

to brush
to comb
to hold

My hair
no longer
in my eyes

Rebecca Hides Her Scar

The affair
was about finding the rest of me.
There were moments when I wanted
to be the other woman I dressed up to be.

When I was a girl
I loved to walk into my mother's room
open the drawers to her dresser,
search for her secrets.

The affair
was something I could place beneath
the scar on my chest.
I needed fingerprints on my flesh.

I needed someone other than Jim.
Is this a crime?
I wanted desire and not death.
This cancer is deeper than guilt.

Maybe it's me that's growing out of control.
Maybe it's this unspeakable love which kills.

When my lover touches me
it feels like the first time...
My body is new again.
Nothing is broken.
Nothing needs repair.

God
I have no prayers and only one breast.
I call my lover's name and he answers.

Dreaming About Katherine Dunham

The sound of their voices
against the bedroom door
is like rain falling next
to the face of Lena Horne.

My husband talks to our daughter
about money, bills, insurance
and stormy weather.

Since the accident
I've been knocked down like a
girl in a high school fight.

In the corner of the room
a wheelchair glistens like a chariot.
Who will now turn around to whistle at my legs?

When the name Jesus slips from my lips
I think about the distance to the toilet
and how being able to take a piss by myself
is a step toward heaven.

Birds

I don't count birds
so when the fourth body hits the floor
I stop counting because it's too easy
shooting people with a gun and besides
I forgot my math book and where it is
is anybody's guess including my own

My daddy placed this gun in my hand
when I was crawling after things crawling
Rabbits
Squirrels
Cats
Dogs
Who cares if they have four legs or two

I just like to aim and shoot and taste the
rush it gives me like the roller coaster
at the fair and the cotton candy and root
beer and the hot dogs and pickles and relish
dripping down the side of my hands

Red spot in my eye but I keep shooting
teachers and kids until the gun clicks
and the fun runs out and I know this
must be the movies because I'm alive
and everyone else is dead

In Shadows There Are Men

We were never absent
or invisible
we were always here

Our lives interrupted
by what others
wanted to see

Sometimes what
we want is the
taste of the kiss
and the touch of
a hand

Even our women
stare at us
disgusted with how
we live

Never knowing
how we struggle
to love

## Geography

My four year old daughter comes home
from school with a map of the world. This
is Africa she tells me. This is where we
come from. Daddy watch me color the rest
of the world. I watch her color Europe red
and all of the Atlantic. I try to encourage
the use of blues and greens but she refuses.
She sees the world with her own brown eyes.
My daughter stops coloring and prints her
name at the top of her map. Jasmine, she
says like a young Columbus. Her mouth
round with wonder.

Liberia Fever, 1877

My youngest comes running
out of the summer nightmare
chased by white men who would
prefer us dead instead of free

When I sleep the same dream
returns like a ship sailing across water
sweating I toss in my bed while my wife.
mumbles a prayer for protection

All our possessions
in our hands
We walk on the same land that planted
scars on our backs and feet

Many folks suffer from a strange fever
Something cured only by the touch of an African
wind

## Anna Murray Douglass

I cannot read the North Star
but it shines at night in my bedroom.
I hold a free man in my arms.
Is it love that still keeps me a slave?
What speech could he whisper in my ears
that would make me listen to his heart?
In the dark does my dark skin remind him
of the darkness?
I cannot spell the word abolitionist.
I can only read the name Frederick Douglass.
I know these two words well.
Many will remember the life he lived.
And me?  Yes, they will say I was his wife
before he married the white woman.

Nothing but a Man

When he turns to sleep on his side
I stare at his back and place my hand
where segregation once was.

If my lover is the black messiah
then tonight I rest his crown on my head.

Martin – I whisper in the dark.
Our presence in this hotel room
is like a candle ready to be knocked over.

Fire spreading like love.
Rumors leaping to a tape recorder
next door.

Crosetti

Frank Crosetti
a gentleman in pinstripes
stands near third base.

How many heroes
will he escort home?

1932 and Ruth looks into
the Cubs dugout,
points a finger and calls
the shot.

A young Crosetti will think
of the Babe when he shakes
the hand of Roger Maris in
1961.

Baseball is a game played
by men who know the silence
of grace and the beauty of
records made to be broken.

A Poem for Richard

At two and three in the morning
when sleep walks away like a lover

I think of Richard Wright
dead at fifty-two

He lived in a small apartment in France
alone without Ellen or the kids

A few days before Wright died
Langston Hughes knocked on his door

Here was the poet of Harlem
saying hello to the black boy and native son

I think about Langston looking
into Richard's eyes and searching for a river

Maybe the Mississippi moving one more day
down the delta with the blues

Alexander Calder
(1898-1976)

I can make
the world move

Bend
Spin
Flutter

Wind kissing wire
Red metal tickling

Air

*XI.*
*The Ear Is an Organ Made for Love*

After Phillis Wheatley Sailed to England

Master took me into town
where the big boats dock.
I stopped loading the wagon
and stared at the water.
The horizon had a familiar
glow. I touched my skin
and remembered chains.

An elder in the Square was
weeping. He said we could
only return home after the
invention of the airplane.
Is this true Phillis?

Until then, must we stand
in the middle of fields
with our arms open?

You Are a Galaxy to Me

A man dreams of a woman's
nakedness and her body becomes
his pillow. He sleeps making love
to her with his eyes closed and
heart open.
There is nothing but desire
in darkness.

A man falls off the world
from loving a woman too much.
Why is there so much space
between bodies?  A man holds
his penis like a star.

Why Is It Greek Omelet and Not Puerto Rican?

Every morning I
look for you on the menu.
Where are
your eyes and lips,
my side order of thighs?

I'm so hungry for the sauce
of you and the way your
blouse opens
like a flame

Autumn
*for W. R.*

The back of your neck
Is a beautiful path for walking
Your hair is falling

Tatum

Show me your hands
If you're Art Tatum

Music keeps sitting
By my window

Some days I just want jazz
To place her tongue in my ear

May 16, 2003

The Lakers lost last night
Kobe crying sweat and tears
at the end of the game. Robert
Horry was horrible. I thought of
Albert Alyer floating near New
York without a horn. Poor Horry
without a note of a shot left in
his hands.

Neruda

*for Naomi*

Neruda's head is across town.
It's in the garden outside
the OAS building.

I need to go there.
No, I need to find what they
did to the rest of Neruda's body.

Where are Neruda's hands?
Legs?  Feet? Did someone believe
Neruda's poems came only from his head?

What does one make love with?
Bring me Neruda's poems!
Ask them to confess.

Tender Zippers

You make me feel zip.
Unzip.
Zippery.
I would love to zip you.
Zip with you.
Zip off with you.
Pull your zipper.
Zip.
Zip.
Zip down.
Don't zip me up.
Zip along with me.
Zip today.
Zip tomorrow.
I want to always zip you.
What's your zip-code?
My hand is on my zipper.
Come play with my tender zipper.
You make my tender zip.
Zip goes my zipper.
Oh, tender zippers!
Oh, tender, tender zippers.

Alone

The streets are empty
without your arms.

Untitled

On your left hand
a paper cut near your thumb.

I notice small things
because I love you so much.

Orange(s)

I bring oranges
and place them near your bed.
Joan Miro is painting a hand
near my heart. So surreal.
Colors the color of oranges.
Should I rent kisses or move into you.
Why are the oranges cut in
half? The lips of your clitoris wet
with juice. I remember the
smell of everything.

Body Armor

Everybody is looking for work
Nobody has money
Somebody always gets paid

Touching a body
Comes with a price

Class Struggle with Wings

Birds fighting for food near my bench.
Why do I feed them crumbs?

The Dark Side

The dark side of the house has undisturbed secrets.
My hands grab rake
and bags. I pull weeds,
stare at them as if they
were confessions—so
many.

The Ear Is an Organ Made for Love
    *for Me-K*

It was the language that left us first,
The Great Migration of words. When people
spoke they punched each other in the mouth.
There was no vocabulary for love. Women
became masculine and could no longer give
birth to warmth or a simple caress with their
lips. Tongues were overweight from profanity
and the taste of nastiness. It settled over cities
like fog smothering everything in sight. My
ears begged for camouflage and the chance
to go to war. Everywhere was the decay of
how we sound. Someone said it reminded
them of the time Sonny Rollins disappeared.
People spread stories of how the air would
never be the same or forgive. It was the end
of civilization and nowhere could one hear
the first notes of *A Love Supreme*. It was as
if John Coltrane had never been born.

So This Is What the Living Do

When did we begin to wear sneakers to funerals
Or sport jerseys and caps?

When did things begin
To die?

I pass a church four blocks from the Safeway.
I see the last generation of old black men in suits.

These men are professionals.
They touch death every day.

They carry the coffin and drive the hearse.
They arrange the flowers and offer comfort.

They escort you into limos and tell you where to sit.
They know the directions to the cemetery.

What do you know?

I know that I am dying.
Dreams first or what you might call the lint of disappointment.

It has always been this way—this knowing.
The realization that I will do this alone.

I once believed in love the way I believed in beauty;
The living with dignity, style and grace.

I thought my shoes always needed to be polished
Whenever I left the house.

There is a way the day ends after you pass a funeral.
How you walk down the street afraid to look over your shoulder.
They say this is what the living do.

Austerity
  *for Temo*

We will all lose our jobs
If not today then tomorrow.

A writer calls me asking about
How to get published. Writers
Are having a difficult time. I start
To explain the journey we are on,
The poet's path. The writer interrupts
Me and says—
*Cut the metaphysical bullshit! I*
*want a Mercedes Benz.*
What do you want?
Today I returned my poems to my lover.
I filed for unemployment.
My heart stopped.

Stone

Maybe next year
we will live with more urgency.

We will love days of dangerous
new beginnings.

I once waited near windows
and doors for your return.

Outside it is October (again),
everything is changing color.

Red, orange, brown.
The leaves are falling.

I remain black.
A small stone for your coat pocket?

I like how your hands hold me.
Maybe you could *skip* me across

the lake and make me believe
it's love.

Excerpts from the Lost Diary of the Black Houdini
         *for Enid Miller*

1.

What if I told you slavery was nothing but a magic trick gone wrong.
Would you believe me?

2.

It was during segregation that I decided to hang myself upside down.
My feet pointing North and upwards—my head still in the South.

3.

There is no prison I cannot escape from.
I've known blackness.

4.

When I was a young boy, I was a runaway.
I disappeared from the plantation and then history.

5.

What is the difference between escape and erasure?
How many times have I changed my name?

6.

The Colorline makes us all acrobats.
I learn to pass white folks without a net.

7.

The crowd applauds after each performance.
When they look into their mirrors they see me.

8.

I taught Marcus Garvey the hat trick.
Everyone loves a parade.

9.

King tells me his dream.
I consult my dream book and find a page missing.

10.

My father takes me to Coney Island.
He tells me all of America is an amusement park. Learn to laugh or die.

11.

Fame made me a Race Leader.
I get paid for describing misery not magic.

12.

White teeth and a big smile.
I hide the key under my tongue

13.

Let me tell you about "Metamorphosis."
It will explain why I'm there and not here.

14.

Love is a pair of handcuffs. Do
I want to escape?  Can I?

15.

My mother died yesterday afternoon.
All my life I've been trying to reach her.

16.

I hold my breath and keep counting.
How long can I survive underwater without love?

Who Turns the Wheel?
*for Charles Johnson*

We dreamers.
Men of night emails and exchanges. Composers
of narratives and American songs.
We believers and followers of the Buddhist path.
We understand the blackness that surrounds us.
We surround the blackness, we follow it
Embracing ourselves.

We are brothers because everything in life
Is related to love. We take refuge in the future
Knowing the past is always found in the present.
Your silver hair filled with the roots of wisdom.
Now the lotus flower blossoms—erasing pain
And suffering.  Paradise is no longer fiction. So many
Waiting to hear from you. Speak. Write.

Red Light and Green Means Go

There are moments when I miss you
or simply wonder what you're doing.
I think of you sad, tired, even alone.
Maybe too many of us love in foreign
languages, which is why our hearts are
always searching for someone to translate a
feeling into something else. There are days
when the only thing I want to do is cross the
street. Why is there always a red light in the
corner of your eye?

I Remember Loretta Young
*for Enid Miller*

I am holding my mother's death certificate.
There are no more secrets between us.
I know the exact time she departed: 3:45 PM.
I even know her Social Security number.
I am holding more than my mother's hand.
On my mother's death certificate her occupation
is listed as homemaker. Who wrote this?
I thought an occupation was what you did when you
left the house. When you went downtown
and punched a time card or carried a briefcase. I thought
my mother was a seamstress, a woman who sewed
rhinestones onto clothes. A woman who worked in a
factory. Maybe my mother only did this when my father
failed as a homemaker. When he could no longer pay
all the bills. When there was a need for more money. Did
my mother change her clothes while I was sleeping? Did
she leave the house when I was at school? Homemaker?
I thought my mother was a housewife.
I thought a homemaker was someone I saw on television.

One day I told my brother and sister that our mother
was Loretta Young. They laughed at me and kept their
secrets to themselves. Now my sister sends me my mother's
death certificate. It comes in the mail with the latest copy
of The New Yorker and a few bills. At the bottom of the document
is the cause of death. All the words have something to do with
the heart. Nowhere do I see the word love. All the boxes
checked are too small.

Cholera

In Haiti
A wheelbarrow

Transports
The dead

The living
Keep pushing

Before Hip Hop

Before
Hip Hop
There was

Nat
King
Cole

Sugar Ray
And
Miles.

Cool
Was
How

You
Held
A

Cigarette between
Fingers or entered
A ring or simply

Found your stage
And turned your back
To the world.

Circus Animal

Another day inside this cage

My life broken into many pieces

I keep cutting myself against the bars

Breath

So you open yourself
And take your heart out

It's still beating

You blow on it to
Make it go faster

Flying

Did you know Flying Africans were seen before the Civil War?
I saw a photograph of Frederick Douglass surrounded by proud black men

It was taken before 1863. Everyone has freedom in their eyes.
One man is wearing a Tuskegee Airman jacket, another an Air Jordan cap.

Lately the wind comes down to watch me stand in the doorway of my cabin
It extends a hand of light when I see nothing but darkness.

The wind tells me to breathe, then flutter.
It tells me to stretch, then rise.


Flying is nothing but memory.

Lessons from Houdini

You practice disappearing
in front of a mirror. All your wife can
see is your face. Magic is how your
body vanished in bed. Once you
practiced with knives and hats.
The rabbit trick was a snap. Houdini
comes back from the dead to explain how
to escape from a trunk underwater. He
tells you to hide a divorce in your
marriage. Learn to pick the lock. Convince
yourself there are no chains. Practice
holding your breath. Count
the years. Surface through the pain.

Sneakers 1995

(In the holy year of our Jordans)

When there were cracks
in our sidewalks

children killed
each other for sneakers.

My neighbor
buried a son barefoot,

a reminder of how
he came into the world.

I looked out windows
late at night

and saw white joggers
running like stars.

I didn't know
they were missionaries

announcing the end
to this sad world.

Meetings
  *for Holly*

I'm sitting in another meeting
where people are talking about money.
They call this fundraising. We spend the time
talking about people who have money.
We mention names of people we don't know. This
is what you do when you don't have money. You
talk about people who do.

Before the meeting ends there is agreement
among everyone to contact three people
who have money.  I leave the meeting knowing
I won't make any calls. I walk down the street
talking to myself. At the bus stop I search
my pockets for money. This too is fundraising.

When the bus arrives all the poor people board.
I'm on my way to another meeting.
The poor people are going to work. A
guy sitting in front of me is yelling
on his cell phone. He is talking about money.

He says—

*I don't give a fuck!*
*I want my fuckin' money!*

This too is fundraising.

Cell Phones

In the days before cell phones
we spent our time looking for loose change.
We ran to the phone.
We tripped over phone cords
or stood on lines waiting to use a phone.
We forgot phone numbers.
We were listed in phone books.
There was no text messaging.

In the days before cell phones
there was phone sex and people slept with their phones.
Phones were big and hung on walls.
You could cradle a phone and wait for a sweet dial tone.
If you were lonely, you could call the operator.
There was always someone to assist you.

Today everyone has a cell phone.
They spend days and nights talking in strange places.
You could be in the middle of reading a poem and—
someone's cell phone will ring.

In the days before cell phones you searched frantically
in your bag trying to find something to write with.
You wanted to find a pen not a phone
before the ringing in your head stopped.

The Killers

1927 and I'm just a Negro in a kitchen.
Will they kill me too?  I got a towel
In my mouth like it's ham and eggs. Sam
they call me, but it's not my name.  Al ties
Nick to me like I'm Sidney Poitier. Two big
killers in a small diner looking
for a Swede. What do they think I know?
Have they lost their Hemingway?
Short stories die young.
Characters try to run.
*The door of Henry's lunch-room opened and two men came in.*

Boxing with Your Mom

*Whoever said men*
*Hit harder when women*
*Are around is right*
                    *— Yusef Komunyakaa*


You push the door open not knowing
what to expect. She sits in a chair next
to her hospital bed. Just sitting. How long?

Before you can even enter the room a big
smile of recognition kisses her lips before
she kisses you. Her seamstress eyes survey

your clothes. You're a rhinestone of a son
slipping between her shaking hands. As the
spark leaves her eyes she withdraws under

her hospital robe. So small she looks. So small
she is. You want to leave but you just came. It's
just you and her. You're overmatched.

Her moods change so quickly you can't avoid
her jabs. There's bitterness in each blow. She
has you against the wall. You're fighting with

her again. This is sick you tell yourself.
You want to leave but the bell never rings.
You're trying to love her too much.

You're losing another round.

After the Flood

In New Orleans
Brenda Marie Osbey is sitting in the lobby of
the Omni Royal on St. Louis Street. Outside
Don Cherry is talking to the whales.

Poems from Notebook

The Lonesome Lover

The lonesome lover hands me
Her card. It reads:

Burial comes with a vacancy.
Walk in beauty on the path to love.



The Soul as Souvenir

A store on Commercial Street
Many Buddhas in the window

A tourist stops and looks for a path
There is only one doorway

The 10 Race Koans

*As presented to Charles Johnson on the morning of July 13, 2008*

Race Koan #1

Why is the cotton white
and the hands black?

Race Koan #2

How come our ears are always open
but we can't hear the sound of freedom?

Race Koan #3

What's the difference between
the Colorline and the starting line?

Race Koan #4

I have a dream
and you have a dream.

Do we share the same dream?

Race Koan #5

Is sitting in the dark
the best way to describe

blackness?

Race Koan #6

A blind black man
boards a bus.
What do you notice first
his blindness or blackness?


Race Koan #7

Do you ever wonder what Stevie Wonder sees?


Race Koan #8

When DuBois called Garvey
"a Negro with a hat"
What was he wearing?


Race Koan #9

When a black fist
causes a black eye
is this Black Power?


Race Koan #10

Red, white and blue.
Red, black and green.
What do colors mean?

The Odyssey of O

Origins omen oracle obvious odd odd-ball odds one
Outsider outrageous obstacles obstinate obstruction
Orator options obligations onlookers
Opponents old guard old school
Operation objectives organize organization overwhelm
Ovation outstanding overcome overdue obtain
Optimism outvote outspend overflow opportunities
Official occupant Oval Office Obama obsidian
Ovations Old Glory open house our O

The End of Civilization as We Know It

You're sitting on the toilet
And turn to discover
There is no more toilet tissue

## Heath Ledger Was Found Dead Yesterday

So I get ready to leave Busboys and Poets around 2:15 in the afternoon
after meeting with Marc, John, Lorrie, Andy and Beth.
Steve our waiter recommended the pecan pie so there
is still a sweet taste left in my mouth. I walk by the bookstore
only to discover—Don is not working today. I look over my shoulder
wondering about all the novels that will go unread.
Oh—there is Lori Tsang standing next to the magazines and the work
of Garcia Lorca. I run over and pull her away from Neruda who wants
to recite another love poem. I hug Lori while humming "Embraceable You."
There is no foul play—just old friends meeting in another city
outside New York.

Letter #4

Dear Micky,

How can you go to the park? Do you remember the colored kid Pumpsie
Green? The Red Sox was one of the last clubs to hire your people. I know.
I got contacts in both leagues. We had a deal to bring in some Cubans
but Fidel spoiled that. Now Micky stay away from ballgames and the
autobiographical essay. So many folks writing them and not hitting their
weight. If you just want to go to the game for a beer and a cap – let me
know. I try to keep everything cold. Once, Ted Williams kept his bat in
my freezer. Kid got three hits the next game. They said he was the greatest
hitter but no one ever knew about the icebox. You have to be real cool to hit
.400. Now Toni Morrison she has speed just like that boy Jackie Robinson.
Beloved, I call both of them. God I can still see him stealing home and
Milkman falling back to earth. God Micky, why don't you just read instead
of sitting behind third base. Wave the other poets home the next time the
World Series hits Boston.


Don Millo

Letter #5

Dear Micky,

What's with the sermon? You sound like one of those colored
preachers. What was the name of the guy who ran for president?
You know the guy who was always talking about how pretty he
was. Was that Clay or Jackson? Anyway, all that stuff you talking
about smells like the sixties. Form is James Brown asking for his cape
back or Ricky Henderson slapping his glove after catching a ball.
Form is Jordan pulling at his shorts and everything else comes from
the blues. Micky, go south and watch the Mississippi chase a dog's
tail. The blues is the essence of black culture. All you have to do is
play, folks think too much Micky. I told Booker T this was going
to happen. Micky, go get your guitar. I can find you a nice place to
play and study. I'll treat you better than Capone did Armstrong.
You remember Louie? Boy could play. Micky, I'm talking form.
Blues baby, just hum and everything will be all right. Now just don't
go back to church on me Micky. I need you in the business. Folks
getting published and no one needs a godfather? Go figure. Too
much color in the world Micky. Too much color. It makes me cry
white sometimes. Sometimes I just form all over my mouth. It must
be the food I eat Micky. I need to hire a colored cook. Talk to me
Micky send me some references. I hear that gal Toi has those black
notebooks. Anything I need to taste? I could use a good poem Micky.
Sometimes to ease the pain, sonnet and tonic. Is that too civilized for
this time of year? I miss the old country Micky. I miss it.


Don Millo

Letter #6

Dear Micky,

See, folks don't understand politics. It's a mind thing, something DuBois didn't understand. Not even Rosa Parks. You want a seat on the bus get your ass on it. Do you think Parks had on the right dress and hat that day? If you dress colored and look colored then folks will treat you like colored. Now Micky, I keep telling you—you the next Langston. You after rap music and hip hop. The next century has to come through your work but you don't know how to pose. We have to place you back on that slave bloc.

Teach your eyes that distant I love Africa look and keep your Mojo straight. Someone mess with your Mojo you in deep trouble. It will take Hollywood and 100 directors to correct it on the big screen. Now your problem is that you play with the ladies too much. You need to get some Zen tea and keep your heart pure. Follow your Mojo Momba and rise. I'm talking about spirits Micky. Pray to the spirits and they will come—they might even bring you one of those lit prizes and an NAACP image award. But don't pray too much Micky—it's bad on the knees.


Don Millo

Letter #7

Dear Micky,

So you only write to me when you have good news? OK. I took those
poems. No more sitting outside the hospital doors. If you can make a person
well—do it. That's what Toni Cade Bambara was talking about in The
Salt Eaters. You remember that important first page—"Don't you want to
be well?" Well that's the question for the 21st century. No more colorline
bullshit. So it's important for my Micky to be well. Let me look out for you.
I want books and prizes for you. Nothing less. If we have to get you a Little
Richard uniform we can play that too. Maybe you too black to win? Are we
back to Ellison? What did you do to be so black and blue? Tell me Micky.
You know everyone was surprised about how that stamp project went.
How did Don Millo pull that off? Folks was calling me a Wizard. Hey—they
need to read Hurston. It's all there in her work. All you have to do is believe
Micky. That's what Lena Horne told Diana Ross in the Wiz—right? Be sure
your eyes are watching God Micky and not the legs of the woman next
door. Problems of the heart are for romance writers. Problems of the mind
are for academics and revolutionaries. Problems of the spirit are what we
have to solve. Find your bowl and love your soul.
That's my advice to black poets. OK Micky? Find your bowl and love your
soul. Everything else is business and a card will take care of that. I got your
back Micky. Just keep writing. It beats picking cotton or working for Mr.
Ford. That's why musicians were so nice to Mr. Capone. He just let them
play. Don't you like to play Micky? Ciao baby—and let Lester leap in.


Don Millo

Emmett Till Looks at a Photo Album from Iraq

Sometimes I try to remind folks that Money
Mississippi was a jail too.

Hoods come in one size.

I look at the pictures in this album
And see myself

Whistling at the lady guard
Who gives the thumbs up.

After the Storm

Cleaning up
after the storm

the flower pot
breaks

How Stories Begin
*for W.R.*

she told him there was
a magic house near the
river. it was where she
lived. one day he left
her body behind and became
mist. he wanted to see her
in the morning when the first
drops of sunlight touched her
fingers. he wanted to be the
moisture on her tongue and
everywhere the earth opened
like flesh.

Divine Love
*for Alexs and Soojin*


I wish I had loved you many years ago.

I would have loved you like Ellington loved jazz and Bearden loved scissors.
I would have loved you like Langston loved Harlem and the blues loved
Muddy Waters.

I would have loved you like Douglass loved to read and Garvey loved parades.
I would have loved you like Zora loved stories and DuBois loved suits.

I would have loved you like Louis loved boxing and Mahalia loved to sing.
I would have loved you like Carver loved peanuts and Wheatley loved poems.

I would have loved you like Jimmy loved Lorraine and Ossie loved Ruby.
I would have loved you like Martin loved Jesus and Malcolm loved Allah.

## XII.
*Falta De Ar*

There Are No Saints Only Lovers

I need someone to take my body
down from the cross. There are holes
in my hands from touching. My feet
like words keep me from leaving.
There are too many questions
of why we failed. I refuse to confess
to love or sin.

Tipping

The tip of my tongue
went looking for you today.

## When Shall I Rise from This Burial?

I felt the lash
this morning

Something more
than hurt or pain

Something closer
to grief

The face of my mother
when her mother died

Like a child separated
from a hand or breast

And knowing nothing
of slavery


There are birthmarks
on my skin

And places where
history's wounds

Are forever
open

Taking Flight with My Imagination

So you're gone—
Up North where I hear there are still abolitionists.
What is love but slavery—
Is freedom still to be found in your arms?
I fear a long winter—a gray sky and much darkness.
Still the thought of you walking across the room naked
brings light to my eyes

The Shortness of Breath

Knees and memories
this is what goes first.
The difficulty of walking
embraced by the inability
to remember. One falls
and discovers the shortness
of breath or how sunlight
enters a room only to be
seduced by shadows.

The Kirti Monastery

*for Tibet*

The monks are setting themselves
on fire. I smell the smoke of their souls.
The rising flames of protest embrace
the world. Death is the forgiveness
of life. Every prayer a match.

Alone

No moon tonight
Empty bed
Pillow on the floor

My Father as Prophet and Provider

*for Egberto Miller*

He did not speak
often. I only heard
him when he spoke.
My fear of him
rewarded my silence.
His love was a gentle
terror. Out of respect
I was always good.
The fierce light in his
eyes a reminder that
my life would never
succumb to darkness.

Tubman
*Arm yourself, or harm yourself*
—*Amiri Baraka*

Short woman with a gun
Leading me through the woods
Footprints left beside rivers

Freedom is a powerful thing
Sometimes you have to hold it
In your hands and listen

For the click

Affairs

All affairs begin in fiction
And end in fiction

Poetry

Early morning — outside the cold air
Turns snow to light

Hot tea
Lemon and honey
A book of poems near my cup

The first sip
A taste of love

I Fall in Love Too Easily

*for Maria*

Like Miles you lean into me
Play the center of my back
With your fingers

Your hair now silver
Touches me like years—

Oh, how the trumpet
Of your lips reminds me of how
Poor I've been without you

Love Is About Forgiveness

Love is about forgiveness—
so I forgive you for being you—for being
beautiful and wonderful (all over) and laughing
and giving birth to poems—for being a friend
that makes me howl whenever I dream
about your nakedness—which is so often
I no longer have words for love—only tears.
Yes, crying is the river I walk near when I
think of you.

Postcards

When was the last time you mailed a postcard?
My mother kept the ones I sent her. My sister mailed them
back to me after my mother died. I had forgotten I had written so
many small notes to my mother. The price of stamps kept
changing. I was always mentioning on the back of cards
I was having a good time. I can remember the first time
I lied to my mother. It was something small maybe the size
of a postcard. I went somewhere I was not supposed
to go. I told my mother I was at the library but I was with Judy
that afternoon. Her small hand inside my hand. I was beginning
to feel something I knew I would never be able to write home about.

Life

There is a ladder in the room
that goes nowhere

Untitled

At the end of the day we learn from our lives and the lives of others
You are either facing a wall or standing against one

# XIII.
## *50 Love Poems for a Friend*

#57

The warm weather
makes me think of you near
water. There are waves
of love yet to touch us.
All the sand falls slowly
through our hands
as if our eyes were clocks
waiting to undress.

#67

You place yellow
flowers on the table.
I stand looking
at your neck, back
and every petal
that is you. Why
are desires cut
like stems?

#78

The heart is a small
room. Too often we
fail to open the window
and let love in.

#85

These are the saddest
lines I will write (this
summer). The ocean
a witness to friendship
and tides. My heart
a seashell as empty
as every night
you are away.

#87

You occupy everything.
There is nowhere
I can go without you.

#97

I live in bright darkness
a place where love goes
to die. The sky of blue
longing. The hand of gray
despair. What grows green
are my dreams of you. The
red nights of passion and
the fruit of words.
Come hold the ash of me.
The black of me now.

#100

I take out the trash
as if my life was a bundle

tied tight at the top—
a knot preventing my head
from falling

out.

So sad the smell of sadness
and the sweet waste of love.

## XIV.
## New Poems

Early Morning at the Temple

Your face
like the smooth stone

on which I wrote my first poem
—words near the river.

Does morning light
open the door to your heart?

Why are our eyes still dark?
Why is our love so late?

Turning the Knob

Spring is opening the door.
I notice her hands
are without gloves.

First Poem

The first poem at a reading
Should always shock and awe

It should be a love poem
Of overwhelming force

Maybe the mother
Of all poems

War reduces everything
To silence

Every soldier's grave a place
Too loud for sleep

Morning

You rise thinking it's just another day.
But the first African is being captured down near the shore.
It's going to be a long history.

Freedom Ride

from the back of the bus
I can hear the wind outside
splashing against the hull

of seats as if this was the
shores of Africa during rush
hour and the slave trade is

steered by a driver who never
learned the words to Amazing
Grace

bless me Father for knowing
the difference between unemployment
and freedom

bless me Father for replacing
chains with change and tokens
and transfers

bless me Father for this window
which turns away the stares
and the eyes filled with despair

bless me Father
as I sit here in the back of
the bus wondering  about the

absence of power and presence

Poem for N

Yes, and then you arrive
and we all go crazy and fall
in love.

The Red Door Loft
                *for Luke*

We are a city of secrets.
Down one street.
Up another.
I walk into an alley looking for music.

Where is the jazz?
Somewhere above
reaching, pulling me up
a twisting staircase?
Is this heaven
or a watchtower?

Bobby (from WPFW)
greets me at the door.
Luke a bass player
is behind him.

$15 buys entrance,
cool air and sound.
Drinks are in the back
there is an ark of people
waiting for the music to flood
the loft.

Time to jump into jazz
with the faithful. Baptize me
behind the red door. To tell
this secret is to love.

Do Tell!

Ear-Up!

Untitled

Don't slip in your own puddle.

## Making My Way Across Town

The bus is going to Duke
Ellington bridge. Is that where
the big bands are?

Elizabeth Alexander writes:
"my life is black and filled
with fortune."

What are the poets doing these days?
I see Holly Bass laughing
with a friend on U Street.

The air is so hot my dreams
are sweating. They could be Louis
Armstrong wiping his brow.

There are days in D.C.
when I wish I had a key
or could invent a door.

H

You leave me thirsty—
If desire is a drink
why should I be tortured
with a straw?

On Meeting Eve a Second Time

You forget
about everything
and the garden
when her blouse
falls open.

God knows
you love
nipples more
than
apples.

Shonda's March

Oils for your hair
when the *word* is given.

The sweet perfume of freedom
falls from your lips.

Let's meet at Harper's Ferry —
John Brown will bless our love.

If we continue to live alone
we die as slaves.

Who Said Love Is Blind?

The bad news still arrives on a slow
boat from somewhere.

People you love are dying along with
people you will never know.

Courts become battlegrounds for marriage
while we wait for hatred to divorce war.

Maybe the sickness in the air
comes from the words we speak.

Press your tears against my eyes
so that I might see you.

A Cold and Trembling Thing

It is the darkness of my cell
at night that finds me clinging
to a sip of prayer and a crumb
of hope. What if I opened my
eyes after 27 years only to
discover I could no longer cry?
What then?

There are laws that must be
broken like stones. I am Mandela
a prisoner on an island.

Why is freedom sometimes
a cold and trembling thing?

The Hooker Never Votes

Politics is a lonely horn
and sometimes I need a woman's
hand to make the pain go away.

Everybody wants something.
But what do I need?
What do I want?

I love the power of flesh
even if it comes with a price.
I'm a politician not a promise.

2 Shorts and a Smoke

I.

Show me your hands
if you're not Art Tatum

Music keeps sitting
by my window

Somedays I just want jazz
to place her tongue in my ear

II.
1967
New York City

Vietnam War
protest

I bump into Paul
Simon without Garfunkel

The rest
is history

III.
Sarah Vaughn is a sweetheart
I'm too young to go steady

All the women I know
have the blues

I'm just a colored
man in love

Water Song

Maybe we should eat our Lester Young.

The rivers around New York are filled
with the ancestors of sick fish I flushed
down the toilet when I was small.

Nothing swims upstream anymore,
there are too many musicians and hookers.

Fools keep being seduced by the sounds of war.
Fuck Peace!

Every woman has a tattoo above her butt and pond.
Even when Sarah Vaughn wasn't naked she could sing.

The war in Vietnam was going on around the time
I saw Jimi Hendrix with a gun in his hand.

After my first piano lesson I wanted to be Cecil Taylor.
My father said I looked more like Art Tatum than he did.

I made love to jazz after school without the safety of an ocean.
I was just learning how to swim.

One day they fished Albert Ayler
out of the river without his horn.

It was the first time I heard silence
and could imitate it.

Tea for Two

For no reason
my mother starts to dance
(with herself).

The music in her head
making things twirl,
twirl, twirl.

I snap my fingers—
I finger-pop!

When my mother—stops
blank recognition
fills her eyes,

hanging like a strap
descending from a shoulder.

Seduction

My mother is sitting by the window
listening to Billy Eckstine on the radio.

For a moment the housework stops
and she is dancing outside.

Dreaming About the Prez

Lester, oh Lester—
you make me feel so
Young.

Dancing With the Dead

You often find yourself holding hands with your shadow.
You know she's secretly seeing someone else.
How long has it been?  You and your shadow.

In every relationship someone is always in the dark.
Just the other day the woman you love was dancing with the dead.
You wanted to know who she was seeing.

You never know when your lover might mistake you for someone else.

One Avocado Is Missing

You sit at the dinner table
eating a meal prepared by your wife.

By this time tomorrow you'll
be miles away maybe even a state or two
beyond the night.

In a few years or a day
you won't be a man or father—
just a memory.

When you look into a mirror
you'll see the scars of statistics—
the face your child will learn to hate.

Relatives will talk about the future without you.
Before and after your name will be
A question mark—maybe a dash as in—gone.

The heavy blues will leave lipstick
on your clothes and everywhere
you turn.

Gone is the food on your plate baby.
That's love stuck between your teeth.

The Five Stages of Grief

Denial:
This has nothing to do with blackness.
This has everything to do with blackness.

Anger:
I could break things
but everything is broken.

Bargaining:
Maybe I should have left
with the slave catchers.

Depression:
I will die in this same skin
that I'm living in.

Acceptance:
Cotton never left the plantation
only my mind did.

The Dark Side

The dark side of the house
has undisturbed secrets.
My hands grab bags
and rake. I pull weeds,
stare at them as if they
were confessions—so
many.

Let Me Know Before My Heart Stops

There must be life on other planets.
I can live without gravity and history.
What was the color of the suitcase Columbus was carrying?
Is that a drone over my poem?
Space is what comes between lovers.
There is a piano in my house I can't play.
It's just a matter of time before the snow is gone.
There is water on the moon.
Nigeria has a new president.
Don't ride the Red Line in DC.
Is the escalator across the street working?

## The Games Children Play

I.

Their teasing stains my shirt. Their looks throw punches at my head.
I hate school. I dodge and run. Maybe I should kill someone.
I keep a notebook filled with doodles. They say I'm talented and have
a gift. They say I might make a name for myself. I carve my name into
my desk. I make a name for myself. I've got a smile for every newspaper
in the world.

II.

Open the school door.
I've got two bags
and three guns.

III.

Point and shoot. Point and shoot. That's all I do. I'm playing tag with
bullets. I'm it. Rebecca who thought I was crazy looks up from her book.
A few days from now reporters will talk about her courage and how
she managed to survive. After she said she didn't love me I kept missing
her. I miss again.

IV.

Is this paint, chalk or blood on my hands? Maybe it's sweat. I feel like I ju
left the gym after making the winning shot.

The Note Taker

It is difficult to determine the exact time
things began to disappear. I have tried.
I have kept a growing list of what is missing:
Phone booths
Mailboxes
Bookstores

In some neighborhoods black people.

I record my observations in notebooks.
The old black and white kind.
The wide ruled. 100 sheets. The type where
inside the cover there is space for a class schedule.

I am learning how to measure words.
A few heavy for tongue and speech.
I have started to sketch. Pictures letting me
see better, perhaps explain. I draw from
memory. A light going on in the back
of my head. I create with a pencil. Ignoring
all lines and borders.

My lips kiss the tip of the eraser.
A farewell to the old life.

There Are Oceans Left to Kill

Now they are shooting holes in all the holy leaders.
But we don't know who they are.
We are trapped between Iraq and a hard place.
A burial ground, a land of insurgents and veils.
Who is shooting whom?
Men die and women die and children die and yesterday someone dropped a dead body
From a car and pulled out a gun and shot the body again and again.
And it didn't matter if it was someone who was Shiite, Sunni or Syrian.
The blood all flows together and lately what was a stream is now a river.
There are oceans left to kill.
There is blood on the windowsill and blood on the floor.
There is blood knocking on the door and blood dancing barefoot in the road
There is blood praying at the mosque and blood calling people to prayer.
There is blood saluting the living and blood burying the dead.
There is blood in Baghdad and blood singing in Babylon.
There is blood on a face and blood on a hand.
There is blood without a head and blood on a knife.
There is blood on me and there's blood on you.
There's blood on the flag and blood on the books.
They are shooting holes into air and into bones and flesh.
They are shooting into dreams and shooting out nightmares.
They are shooting soldiers and they are shooting fools.
They are shooting into schools and shooting out wombs.
They are shooting mothers and cousins, grandfathers and aunts.
They are shooting uncles and brothers, sons and lovers.
They are shooting daughters and sisters and shooting each other.
There is no death left.
There are no trees.
There is no wind.
There is no breeze.
There is just a hole the size of life.
A hole the size of death.
There is only one coffin left.
Now who will stand in line to wait to die?

Who will wait to be shot?
Who will wait to kill?
Who will call the doctor?
Who will pay the price?
Who will make the sacrifice?
Whom should we forgive?
What sinner will confess?
Which God made this mistake?
What night now finds its end?
What day is this that breaks?
What more can we endure?
What bird no longer flies?
What man no longer loves?
What silent heart must learn the song of peace again?
And sing again, and dream again, and come again.

Untitled

Why do we recycle war
but never peace?

The Genesis of Torture

In the beginning
We will all wear black hoods

Our faces will be hidden from history and
Someone will tie a cruel footnote to our genitals

It will be a neighbor disguised as God

What Do They Do?

What do torturers do when they return home?
Do they make love to their wives and play with their kids?
What hobbies do they have?
Do they wash the car and take out the trash?
Do they change their underwear?
What do torturers see when they look in the refrigerator?
When shopping do they go to the front of the line?
Do they get discounts on meat?
Do torturers remember their anniversaries?
Do they place candles on birthday cakes and blow them out?
When torturers go to church who do they pray to?
When they get caught in traffic jams do they curse the cars in front of them
Do they worry when they get dirt and blood under their fingernails?
What type of deodorant do they use?
When torturers leave a room do they turn out the lights?
Are they superstitious?
Do they avoid stepping on sidewalk cracks?
Do they read their horoscopes before going to work?
How many torturers have two jobs?
When lost do they ask strangers for directions?
Are they left-handed or right-handed?
Do torturers sit in outdoor cafes and talk about torture?
Do they suffer memory loss?
Do they call in sick and say they can't report for work?
How safe is a torturer's workplace?
When they fall to sleep do they snore?
Do torturers keep everyone awake at night?

My Lebanon, My Love
*War surrounds us but I'm taking the day off.*
—Hind Shoufani

Beautiful Beirut
please tell me someone overslept
and a bomb did not explode today.

Tell me the smoke
is not my lover's perfume.

Let us sit in cafes
with tea, coffee and conversations.

I want to say hello
to a woman's lips.

Is that a comma near her legs,
a period near her breasts?

Did you know beauty is now
a refugee?

Desire said I would never
see home again,

Hind—is this true?

Does war now surround
every heart?
Or is it simply our loneliness
that sleeps with separation.

I miss you.
I miss days of love
and peace.

The Widow of Baghdad

After another funeral
the widow removes her black dress
and turns it over to darkness

where

it hangs itself in the corner of the room.

Turning to look into her mirror
she discovers a lump in her breast—
a bomb resting in her hands.

In Baghdad even soft things explode.

A husband's smile sleeps on a sidewalk
glass glittering instead of teeth.

When the Cherry Blossoms Die

In the picture I am in the third row, one of three black faces.
The newspaper lists my name and age.
I find comfort knowing everyone is younger than me.
I am among the 25 shot and killed.
I am not among the wounded or the broken.
My eyes are now filled with dusk.
It was the bullet entering my head from behind that whispered to me.
The shooter found me hiding under a table.
It's what adults did when the only fear came from Russia.
Every teacher told us to turn our eyes away from the windows.
The second bullet reminds me of Nagasaki.
It blinds my life into darkness.
I sleep hearing only Japanese.

Going to Meet the Butcher

Soldiers walking around Walter Reed
Hospital with no legs. Your whole child
missing. You remember how you told
him to always wear a hood. He was eight
the year that winter snow fell and created
long lines at the stores. You gave him a
big bill for his pocket. You needed meat
for the stew. Just get what looks good
baby. It was the first time you sent your
child to meet the butcher. Now a man is
holding a sharp knife behind your flesh
and blood. He recites the ingredients of
war. God is great he proclaims. I'll trade
you a head for a country.

Is This the History of Air?

"I can't breathe " he said.
But there was no air.
Only the absence of trees
and rope.  The swaying
of history over another
black body.

## 5 Shards of Whiteness Cutting into Blackness

1.

An empty seat next to a black person
on a crowded bus. White people
standing but not too close. Welcome
to the fear of sitting.

2.

Coins drop from white hands
into black hands. Thank God for gravity.
It keeps one from touching.

3.

Black bodies waiting patiently in line
in front of a counter. Suddenly—a white
person arrives and goes to the front of the line.
No excuses and no excuse. Blackness is a red
hot coal. Best to stand back and not get burned.

4.

No matter how intelligent the black words are
the white ears will only talk about the rhythm.
The sound of it—that dancing sound. Oh – that
drum—that banjo and those plantation days.

5.

In a business room a black voice speaks
and makes several excellent points.
Seconds later a white voice explains
what the black voice was "trying" to say.
Everyone listens to the echo.

Still Life in Black

Outside the museums black
homeless men sleep on benches

Black plastic bags their only
possessions

The Cutting Edge
*for Bovery*

Democracy
is not paper.

It is something
living

at times
bleeding (but free).

The artist
must take

a knife
to the world.

Miller's Law

Knowing one's audience
is the first rule of a lynching.

Looking into the Future

Dear J,

My eyes are tired. Funny how you should be the first
to notice. I guess this is what happens when a man and woman
look at each other on computer screens. Eyes meet and hold
their own conversation. I hear rumors about how they share
poems and stories. There is too much jealousy in the world.
Words are a sad sight for ears. It is difficult at times to
hear or taste destruction. So much noise comes from torture.
Many are pushed into violence and cruelty. My nose is tired
from smelling corpses; my body tired from embracing widows
and playing with children who lack arms. Should I close my eyes
to genocide? My heart will listen to confessions. My faith waits
for you to undress. To be tired is to desire a deep sleep and within
desire is the memory to love (again).

Snow Falling

Snow falling and suddenly you're Bigger
on a rooftop. You once had dreams
about flying an airplane – now you look
at the dice of life and realize the only
gamble left is to leap. Your name
is Miller not Milkman. You are no
longer a Flying African. Who are you?
The question haunts you as much as
the feathers on your arms.

Sardines

Why do we permit our minds
to be placed inside small cans?

If My Blackness Turns to Fruit

Dear America, my love.
If my blackness turns to fruit
do not pull it from the vine;
let it grow from earth to sky
untouched by hateful hands.
So sweet, my juice, my jazz,
my blues, so sad but true.
Dear America, my love.

Look behind your prison walls.
Count the black seeds behind bars,
the cells where nothing blooms.
Can hope flower from despair?
Yes, America, my love,
resistance comes and then the rain.

## When Freedom Comes

Nat Turner knocking on my door.
I'm just a house negro with a spoon.

Falling

One slip and the sky
cracks like bone.
Nothing heals after
death. Snow falling
is the white you
remember. Loneliness
becomes the shadow
to growing old. Where
is the resting place
for black?

Untitled

Some folks never look down after they fall.
They only look up.

Bowl

And then mindfulness enters the mind and for a moment nothing matters except the cutting...
I prepare a salad for dinner. A simple meal. Food fitting into one bowl. Leaves of lettuce, red peppers, yellow peppers, onion, avocado, tomato, basil, oregano, black pepper—Italian dressing. A short prayer and then the movement of fork to mouth. The chewing and the taste of goodness. Then the small act of giving thanks to the bowl for sharing.

Baseball

Let me sit in the ball park
cap turned backwards and
praying for a rally. I need
the sun and sweat to remind
me how much I love the game,
how each year it comes down
to the last inning, the final out.

Fix Something That Is Broken
                    *for Me-K*

When you rise
fix something that is broken.

It will make a difference
between yesterday and today.

Repair your heart
before you love.

Touch another person
with hands that whisper

(or kiss).

*About the Author*

E. Ethelbert Miller is a writer and literary activist. He is the author of several collections of poems and two memoirs. In April 2015, Miller was inducted into the Washington, D.C. Hall of Fame.

*About the Editor*

Kirsten Porter is a freelance editor, poet, and English professor. In 2013, she earned an MFA in creative writing from George Mason University. A dog rescue enthusiast, Porter devotes much of her time to caring for those without a voice. She resides in Northern Virginia and teaches creative writing and composition at Marymount University.

*About the Cover Artist*

Felix Angel was born in Colombia and is an award winning artist. He is known internationally for his art which has been featured in more than one hundred solo exhibitions and nearly 450 hundred group exhibitions, invitational events, art fairs, and biennials across the Americas and Europe. Angel earned an architecture degree from the National University of Colombia and has resided in Washington, D.C. since 1977. www.felixangel.com

APR 2 1 2016

CPSIA information can be obtained
at www.ICGtesting.com
Printed in the USA
LVOW12s1531060416

482439LV00002B/331/P